Gord

T

GORDON MACLELLAND

TWO HATS

A GUIDE FOR THOSE COACHING
OR THINKING OF COACHING THEIR
OWN CHILDREN.

FOREWORD BY HARRY REDKNAPP

© Gordon Maclelland – Working With Parents in Sport
ISBN 978-1-9163621-2-3

First printed 2020

Published by FCM PUBLISHING
www.fcmpublishing.co.uk

Layout and Typesetting by Red Cape Production, Berlin

CONTENTS

CHAPTER 6
Managing "Pre Match Conversations"

CHAPTER 7

CHAPTER 8

CHAPTER 9

ACKNOWLEDGEMENTS

This book has been such an exciting undertaking and with nothing else like it on the market or in the coaching world, the support it has received from the sporting industry is beyond anything that I could have ever anticipated.

I would like to thank Nick Levett and Chris Chapman from UK Coaching, Will Roberts and Emily Reynolds from the Youth Sport Trust and Dan Cottrell from Rugby Coach Weekly for their valued support and guidance throughout the project.

This book has been brought to life by the amazing array of interviewees who have committed so wholeheartedly to be part of this and could not have been more generous with their time and providing such valuable insight for our readers. A huge thank you to you all!

With so many different sports represented and contributions from all over the sporting world, there are a number of people who I need to thank for using their networks to put us in touch with all the relevant people. So, a special thank you to Denise Lewis and Kevin, Sue Anstiss MBE, Kate Porter, Nick De Luca, Simon Toole, Simon Ord, Lee Hogarth, Gavin Grenville-Wood, Lauren Asquith, Gary Laybourne, Martha Lourey-Bird, Kevin Renshaw and Charlie Ford.

A final thank you and the icing on the cake and that is to Harry Redknapp who has given his support to the project by contributing the foreword.

You have all made this such a pleasure to produce and hope that you share the excitement that I have in releasing this to sporting communities all over the world.

FOREWORD
Harry Redknapp

What a fantastic idea for a book and totally unique in the sporting world. I have absolutely loved my coaching and management career and certainly look back with happiness on the moments I spent coaching my own children.

There are no doubts that there were plenty of highs and lows for both my boys, Mark and Jamie and certainly in the case of managing Jamie. I was one of the fortunate few to have coached my child in a professional environment.

To many this would present its own unique challenges, but I am delighted to say that Jamie and myself look back fondly on that time together.

There will no doubt be some difficult moments along the way for all parent coaches but if you remember that you are family and having support from a wider family network, it will allow you to navigate these challenges together.

We have many happy memories from that time and certainly enjoy retelling some of the stories now together.

It is a great privilege to be part of this project alongside so many leading figures from across the sporting world covering such a wide range of sports. It is certainly enlightening seeing so many similarities across sports in terms of coaching your own child as well as some of the uniqueness that each sporting environment can provide.

Gordon MacLelland and his team "working with parents in sport" have done such a great job in putting this together and I hope that it will provide much needed insight and support to sporting organisations, coach education departments and parent coaches throughout the world.

I wish you all the very best with your coaching journey.

> **"** *I find that coaching my own child has been a great bonding experience for both of us and sharing something we both love has had such a positive impact on us both."*

INTRODUCTION

A large number of parents across all sporting communities have coached or are currently coaching their own child, something that will continue to happen within the coaching industry. These amazing parent volunteers are the bedrocks of our sporting community and give up their time, not just to coach their own child but more often, a whole team of children.

It's interesting how parents become coaches. Often it's a voluntarily decision, one made without really understanding what it may entail, but for others, they are pushed or have fallen into the role as there are no other volunteers. There is a big jump from back garden playing, giving a few tips to then formally coaching your own children. Without even realising however, we may have already started our coaching journey.

From the moment we start to play with our children, before adding a bit more structure to their play, to giving them a few pointers our coaching has already begun.

This could be happening to you whether or not you have a personal pedigree in the sport or have a qualification.

It is going to be a varied path where the common bond is the desire to support our own children.

Do not forget that our primary role is to parent regardless of the coaching role that we may end up taking on.

Without the work of these parent coaches, many sporting organisations would be unable to function and sport at grassroots level would have a significant challenge. It would deny many children and not just their own, an opportunity to develop a healthy relationship with physical activity. The commitment we see from parent coaches on a regular basis is phenomenal.

This book explores some of the challenges they face on a daily and weekly basis, the complexity of the relationships with their own children, other siblings and spouses and their relationship with other parents.

Later in the book we hear from a number of leading figures from the world of sport, who have also experienced and faced the many challenges associated with coaching your own child. They also provide some golden words of wisdom based on their experience to pass on to all coaches.

Taking on the role of coaching your own child and other children can be both daunting and demanding. It requires a certain mindset as there will be a huge time commitment, a mindset to do the role as positively as possible, which means engaging in ongoing learning opportunities to enhance knowledge and for some, a whole new range of communication, conflict resolution, management and logistical skills that are not normally used to in their day to day lives.

Whilst we support sporting volunteers and parent coaches for giving up their time, we also feel that people who take on the role need to commit to self-improvement and acquire knowledge in child development and coaching.

The impact that all coaches can have on young people is huge and working with their parents as part of the team can go a long way to helping a child start to develop their full potential, both as a person and an athlete.

Your club and sporting organisation should support you with ongoing training and continued development opportunities.

There can be huge advantages to coaching your own child as you are in a better position than most to know their strengths and weaknesses, both physically and emotionally. I remember fondly my own father coaching my 'mini rugby' team; and can still picture him in what would now be a very uncool tracksuit, being so supportive and encouraging of every young person that he came across, who wanted to play rugby regardless of their ability.

Thousands of coaches navigate coaching their own child successfully every year, but we can all learn and evolve together either in our coaching, our relationship with our own children and in our relationship with other parents and coaches.

We hope that the chapters that follow will give you confidence, support and practical strategies to use immediately that will enhance and provide an amazing experience for you and your children.

I want to take this opportunity to thank all of our experts from the world of sport for their valuable input into this book, I'm delighted that we were able to cover such a wide range of sports from football to volleyball.

" *Best part is seeing my young child developing not only technically but mentally. I think this is rewarding."*

CHAPTER 1
Have Some Conversations

As a coach of 20 years, from every level from u7's right through to adults, I have often wrestled with the idea of coaching my own children. Some days I thought it was a better idea than others and often found myself questioning whether or not I had made the right decisions.

In the end, I decided that I wanted other people to take on this role as I know my own personality, how my normal week pans out and I wanted to enjoy taking on purely a watching brief.

That of course didn't mean that I wasn't playing in the garden, setting up fun games and challenges with my children, I was just keen that I handed them over to others to have a different voice to mine.

Our house is constantly filled with sport either in the garden or on the TV and I was determined that both my children heard about sport from a different perspective, rather than just my own.

However, all the best laid plans went out of the window as I coached my son at school for a year in tag rugby, football and cricket. It was an enlightening experience.

Looking back, I have no doubt that I was extremely demanding of him, more so than I was with the other children and I struggled with managing how the involvement of my own child was perceived by others in the group and parents.

I still loved seeing him develop as a person and certainly enjoyed refereeing the matches he was involved in. It was great getting a close-up perspective of his friendship group, watching him interact with his friends and see and hear what was really important to him.

After the year he moved on and I am yet to take on the challenge again. Who knows, I may well take up the mantle again in the future but for now I am simply just Dad (with the odd bit of input from the side).

BEFORE YOU START – HAVE SOME CONVERSATIONS

You are about to embark on a role that it will have a huge impact on the people closest to you. There will be a considerable effect to your own children, your partners and potentially your own parents if you take on the role and there are a number of conversations that you need to have with a number of different people.

The first set of questions are for yourself.

SHOULD YOU COACH YOUR OWN CHILD?

Well it depends. Do you feel that you can separate the 'Two Hats' of being a parent and a coach? There is more about this in the next chapter but this is the biggest consideration.

As a coach you may need to stretch your child, give them feedback and perhaps criticise and this role may well conflict with your primary role of being a parent, where we love unconditionally.

If you don't feel that you can separate the two roles, then the answer is probably NO. However, if you feel that you can get the balance right or at least feel that you will learn on the job and have this mindset then it may be all systems go.

WILL IT FIT WITH MY NORMAL WORKING WEEK?

With any form of coaching there is often a huge time commitment. Along with training sessions, time will be spent planning training sessions, reflecting on progress and previous matches, organising equipment, sending messages around logistics and dealing with enquiries from other parents often at unsociable times. You may spend less time at home and family time will be effected. If you feel that you can manage this, and it works for you in your context then it is all systems go.

WILL IT AFFECT MY RELATIONSHIP WITH MY OTHER CHILDREN? (IF YOU HAVE THEM)?

It is unlikely that you will have other children involved in the same group that you coach. It will also mean that for a large part of the year you will be unable to spend as much time watching your other child train and play. Will that affect your relationship with them and is your partner or other family members happy to support you?

CAN I DO THE JOB ON MY OWN OR MAY I NEED SOME HELP?

If you feel that you want to do the role but worry about missing some training or games due to other commitments, then there may be another parent who wishes to share the role with you. We would encourage you to consider this and talk about it later in the book.

HOW WILL THIS AFFECT MY RELATIONSHIP WITH OTHER PARENTS IN MY CHILD'S GROUP?

Do you know the other parents in the group that you are thinking of coaching socially? Will you be able to establish clear boundaries with them, just like you will be having to separate your parent and coaching hat? Are you in a position to be objective about all of the decisions that you make regarding the group?

One of the biggest challenges you may face from other parents is the perception of favouritism. This will always exist, but it can be managed much easier if you can clearly be objective. It may be worth you asking yourself reflective questions such as "would I have allowed another player to get away with that?" "Would I have given another player this role with same skills?" "How much match time does my child get in comparison to other players?"

HOW MAY THIS AFFECT THE RELATIONSHIPS OF MY CHILDREN AND THEIR FRIENDS?

Will your role affect the relationship of your child with their friends? Do you know some of them already? Do you get on with them well enough to allow your new role to withstand some of the pressures you may face?

Are they the type of children who will be able to separate you from their teammate or can you potentially see some friction?

You are taking on this role for yourself but also to have a positive impact on your own child and the relationship that you have with them.

AM I WILLING TO SPEND TIME TRAINING AND ENHANCING MY OWN KNOWLEDGE?

A coach's impact on young people can be huge and this role should not be taken on lightly. You should want to commit to improving your own technical and tactical knowledge, your awareness of child development and to enhancing your communication skills are good starting points. Just because we are volunteers does not mean we shouldn't be trying to do the best job that we possibly can.

The second set of questions are for you and your children.

DO YOU WANT ME TO COACH YOU?

This seems an obvious one, but many parents take on the role without having a proper discussion with the child that they are coaching. The key here is really listening to their response and taking on board their body language and responses. If it really is making them upset or anxious, then perhaps it may not be the greatest idea.

Many younger children are unlikely to say 'No' as it will be pretty cool for them that their parent may be involved. However, as they become older their mindset may change considerably, so a regular check in will be important.

DO YOU KNOW WHAT THIS MAY LOOK LIKE?

Whilst your child may think it is "cool", you need to make them aware of some of the potential issues in advance. Most notably that at home you are a parent, and, in the sports environment, you are the coach. This may mean that there may be a different dynamic in your relationship to the one that they are used to. You need to help prepare them for this, there is more on this in the next chapter. This also goes two ways with how they treat you during coaching and match sessions. You could agree that they call you coach the same as other children to allow for the distinction.

ARE YOU HAPPY FOR ME TO COACH YOUR BROTHER OR SISTER?

If you have another child, you need to speak with them to see if they are happy about the plans. Jealousy and resentment in any family dynamic is not good. If you can already have a plan in place that reassures them or explains the level of support that they will get from you and other family members, it may make this conversation easier to handle and they are more likely to be supportive of you and their sibling.

The third set of questions are for you to ask your partner and other family members.

ARE YOU HAPPY FOR ME TO TAKE THIS ON?

Check in with your nearest and dearest as the role will have an impact on the usual family dynamic. You will spend more time absorbed in your phone organising different bits and pieces, you will be away from home more often and at times it is likely to be on your mind. You need to have their support as they will often pick up some of the slack for you around home life.

You may also want to check in with your parents and your closer family network. Many whole families are involved in supporting, providing a taxi service as well as childcare around a young person's sporting experience. At some point in time you are probably going to need to rely on them.

DO YOU THINK I CAN DO THIS?

Your partner and closest family members know your personality traits better than anyone else. They are also likely to be extremely honest with you. Talk to them about it and see what they really think? Some may give you areas or issues to think about that you have not even considered.

Finally, consider asking advice from other sports coaches who have also been through the same experience. They will be able to share personal stories with you and probably be able to provide you with the greatest insight into the experience.

Once you have had these conversations you will be in a much better position to decide if the role is right for you now. Hopefully, it will be as we need as many parents involved as possible in the youth sports space.

Now read on to find out how you can do the job in the best way possible.

- Have some quality conversations
- Speak to your own children, other parents, your wider family and other parent coaches

As a coach consider
- In your own mind can you separate the two roles?
- Do you think you will be able to be fair and objective to all players including your own children?
- Will you be able to give the role your full time and commitment?

As a parent consider:
- Will this work for you and the rest of the family?
- How it may affect my children's relationships with me and their friends
- Am I confident that I can separate the two roles?

❝ *Sometimes, it can be difficult spending quality time with my child, but coaching them has given us a shared experience which we have really enjoyed.*"

CHAPTER 2
Separating the Hats

The most difficult balance that you are going to face is separating your 'parent role' and your 'coach role'. In researching for this book, this is the one area that parent coaches felt they had needed to work really hard on maintaining the balance. No one claimed to get it right immediately and many felt they were constantly reviewing and tweaking it as they went along.

To be an effective parent coach you need to find methods that work for you and your family dynamic.

Your primary role is still that of a parent, to love unconditionally and be there to offer huge amounts of emotional support.

Your coaching role, whilst still encompassing the above, requires you to let go and try to treat your child in the same way that other coaches would treat them, maintaining the same rules and boundaries as the other children in the group.

You will need to be as objective as possible and show no favouritism towards your own child. At times you will need to criticise and give them feedback in public (as you would any other child). This might be something that you are not normally used to doing.

The conversation with your child prior to taking the role is key here as they need to understand that this may well happen but when you get back home, you will revert to being mum or dad.

You need to establish times when you are the parent and times when you are the coach, turning the tap on and off without fail at the right times. Perhaps using the car journeys or when you enter the changing area or venue as the trigger to when you change roles. Agree to only speak about their performance after training and not at the dinner table.

There is a danger that you can get sucked into the role, taking over the whole week and impacting the entire family dynamic and conversations that go on at home. You will spend plenty of time with your child at practise and on match day, bringing it back into the home environment can be too much overload for both you and your child.

Inevitably, talk will turn to the sporting experience for you and your child at home at some point, as we are all passionate and enthusiastic about it and it is a shared interest. However, in an ideal world we want our children to be multi-faceted individuals with many strings to their bow so that they thrive in whichever environments, sports or hobbies that they finally decide on pursuing. We need to be conscious of that and allow them to lead the conversation and also limit this talk time.

From the moment you leave the car to the moment you get back into it after the event, the coach hat is on and you expect your child to follow the same rules and boundaries established with all of the other players.

At home you could agree with your partner to give you some kind of signal or cue when you are playing coach at home or that they feel that conversations are getting dominated by the sporting experiences. Partners can be very good at remaining objective and bringing an impartial view to the situation.

Home Sweet Home is such an important place for families and children and we must do all that we can to keep it that way. Home should be a place where everyone feels safe, a place where our children can vent their frustrations and anger, where they can be themselves and not feel under any extra pressure. Being upset is a stage we go through as we learn to manage our emotions; don't try and 'coach' a short-cut. Allow this to happen and be the parent afterwards.

It should also be a place where we can have great conversations with them and somewhere we are not judging our children, they will get plenty of that out in the big world.

At some point sooner or later, the parenting and coaching hats will collide. Your partner is going to be key here whilst you wrestle the conflict of wearing two hats at the same time. Your child will certainly gravitate towards them at this stage as they will require the parenting "arm around the shoulder."

However, following some of the tips above you can try to keep these moments to the bare minimum. If it does happen, take a moment to reflect, speak with your partner and come up with a agreed plan for the next time either of you spot the danger signs.

- Have some strategies in place for 'separating the hats'
- Come up with a plan that works for your whole family in your own family dynamic
- Speak to your nearest and dearest to help prompt you when you may be overstepping the boundaries

As a coach consider:
- When the coach 'hat' is going on and off
- Have a conversation with your own child about what the coach 'hat' may look like for them and how it may be different to normal
- Let your children know that being their parent will always come first

As a parent consider:
- When the parent 'hat' is coming on and off
- Not formally talking too much about the sporting experience back at home
- Are you making 'home sweet home' with your own attitudes and behaviour

" I am conscious that I am often far too harsh on my own child. I only do this to ensure it looks like I am being fair and treating everyone the same."

CHAPTER 3

Positives of Coaching Your Own Child

There are a huge number of positives from taking on the role of coaching your own child.

First of all, it allows you to spend some quality time with them and share hopefully many happy and memorable experiences. So many great stories, told many years later by parents and their children are based around some of these sporting experiences.

Anecdotally, they remember some of the biggest wins, the dramatic losses, some of the fall outs they had with each other and probably more than most many of the funnier moments of which there will be plenty as you share this journey with your children.

You know your child better than anyone else and as a result of this hopefully you can help motivate, inspire and help support them emotionally during the better and tougher times of the sporting experience. You are also best placed to notice their mood swings; react to them and understand how they may be feeling at any given point in time.

You are in a unique position to also establish some amazing role modelling up close and for your child to see through your coaching, how you behave and what you truly value. We know that children take their lead from us and are always watching our little behaviours and how we handle certain types of situation. In this role they will get a real insight and see it up close and personal more than most.

You need to make sure that you are valuing the things that are truly important. Yes, results can be important, but your impact will be felt far more by your players and parents in developing great people. Emphasising and valuing key character skills such as determination, resilience, good communication, creativity, adaptability and self-organisation would be a brilliant starting point.

The way you conduct yourself on a regular basis, the way you communicate with others and crucially how you behave on the side-line will role model so many key values and have a positive impact on the group that you coach if it is done effectively.

Many parents enjoy the social aspect of being involved in their child's sporting experiences and undoubtedly expand their own personal social network. I am sure that this will certainly be the case for you with the parents close to your group and with other coaches, parents and administrators involved in the clubs you are part of. This can have such a positive impact on our own wellbeing and often opens up so many different avenues in our own lives.

I have no doubt it will also enhance your own development as an individual. You will learn new skills, be put in new situations and, despite not always showing it, there will be an awful lot of people who will be incredibly grateful for you for taking on the role.

You will not just potentially be having a huge impact on your own child's experience but on many other young people and that will be priceless!

KEY POINTS

- Set the tone, be an outstanding role model
- Use all you know about your children to enhance the experience for them
- Enjoy your own self-development as an individual

As a coach consider:
- The way you conduct yourself and communicate with others
- Emphasising the key skills of character development as well as wanting to be successful with the sport
- How your children may be feeling on a given day? Do you need to change your approach?

As a parent consider:
- Making sure you enjoy every moment of your quality time together
- Ensuring that the experience is positive for your own children with regular check ins
- Setting boundaries with other parents particularly if you spend lots of social time with them as well

❝ *We all love to see our children develop and grow as sports people and individuals and coaching them has allowed me to see this improvement firsthand."*

CHAPTER 4
Challenges of Coaching Your Own Child

Unfortunately, there are also a number of challenges that may be faced when coaching your own children.

Firstly, that you can become so engrossed in the experience that it takes over absolutely everything. Trying to manage your own emotions, feelings, logistics and the rest of your family life can take its toll. You need to ensure that you are well organised and have a really good structure in place. It is also vital in managing your own child that the whole experience does not become about you and that their best interests are always in the forefront of your mind.

This extends to the home environment and the back garden, so that every sports session does not become an extra coaching and the 'coaches' hat' starts to appear at the wrong time.

Secondly, everything that you do will be judged by other parents around you and on many occasions perceptions may indeed be wrong. There is a danger that no matter what you do, in trying to be objective, that some other parents will always feel that you are showing some favouritism towards your own child.

In your fear of these external perceptions there is a tendency that you may treat your child differently to the rest. Many coaches say that they have been harsher on their own child when giving feedback to them, often making an example of them in front of the other children and parents.Whilst you may feel that this goes some way to avoiding perceptions of favouritism, this could be damaging the one person that you wanted to support in the first place. A number of coaches have told us that they have deliberately not given their children man of the match or end of season awards, even though they have probably deserved it on merit.

Others have discriminated against their own children over game time in matches and tournaments, keeping them off the field in order to avoid any potential conflicts with other parents.

Awareness is key and this is what we hope the advice in this book is helping to provide.

In some cases, this extra desire to portray fairness is understandable in the hope that it may avoid face to face conflict and send a clear message to the rest of the playing and parent group.

However, there are a number of coaches who show no real awareness of this and without realising can deliberately favour their own child and this can cause unrest amongst other members of the group .

Thirdly, that you use the experience to fulfil some of your own failed ambitions. This can lead to real conflict with your own child. If you want success more than your child, there is the potential that your relationship can suffer. The sporting world has changed dramatically in recent times compared to when we grew up and a different approach is required. Always remember that children's sport is a very different beast to the professional game that we watch on TV.

One of the most difficult challenges is that during training and matches you over analyse what your own child is doing. If you have been a parent before a coach you will be conscious that you tend to watch your child the most, but if you do this as a coach you may well miss things and the opportunity to give productive feedback and encouragement to other players.

It may also lead you to being hyper-critical of your own child as your analysis is so up close and personal. Just because you are there and your child's coach it does not mean that they will not make hundreds of mistakes in learning and getting better, you do not need to pick them up on everything.

We send our children off to school, where they will fail and make mistakes all the time and through this learn and gain valuable experiences and how to make better decisions. The positive is we rarely get to hear about it as it is all part of the process. Have this in the back of your mind when you are coaching.

We need to try and ensure that if we have close friendships with specific members of the parent group that we are coaching that this does not spill over into the experience that we provide all players. All too often as coaches we can feel pressurised by parents, particularly those that we may see as friends, into making far from objective decisions, much like we have been talking about being wary of when it comes to our own children, we also need to bear this in mind . Try to maintain a transparent approach at all times.

This can cause resentment and is a sure-fire way of creating cracks in the sporting group. You need to tell your friends that there can be no special treatment and that you would appreciate if they did not put you in difficult situations along the journey.

Finally, your child will often have to arrive first and leave last as you fulfil your role. The novelty of this can soon wear off, particularly if things have gone badly or the weather is miserable.

Try to make them feel valued at this time, give them some set jobs to do to help you out in terms of setting up or give them a couple of challenges to do whilst they wait

Undoubtedly, the biggest of these challenges is the perception of other players and parents and in the next chapter we are going to look at some potential solutions to help manage this, as well as look at some other useful tips to get you on the right footing.

- Do not let the sporting experience take over every aspect of your home life
- Be aware that your child will be first and last to leave – have some useful things lined up for them
- Ensure you are not using the experience to fulfil some of your own failed sporting ambitions

As a coach consider:
- Be prepared that all your decisions will come under some form of scrutiny
- Try not to focus too much on watching your own child in training and in matches
- Be as consistent and objective as you can in your behaviours and what you are communicating

As a parent consider:
- Manage your emotions the best that you can, do not allow them to spill over into home life
- That our social friendships should not be influencing the decisions that we make as coaches
- That we will not always be able to please everybody including at home

" *My biggest challenge is expectations of my child. Having been a professional in the sport I played I know the attributes and requirements to succeed. This can be a negative as expectation are always high as well as the standards I set."*

CHAPTER 5

Starting As You Mean To Go On

There are a number of things that you can organise and have in place to ensure that this journey as a Parent Coach runs as smoothly as possible. Here are a few things to think about.

SECTION 1 – SETTING UP THE SEASON

Have a Co-Coach or Assistant

A co-coach at this stage could be a really valuable asset and someone who could also help share the weekly burden. If you do have a co-coach it is important that you set up clearly defined roles for each of you both in and out of sessions. This will help provide clarity for all parties.

There can be a danger of too many voices at certain times which can often lead to misunderstandings and confusion. An example of this is at half time that one coach has his say, followed by the co-coach. Sometimes, these messages can be conflicting, they can be the same but are the same delivered by a different voice and half time is spent with the players being bombarded with information.

A solution is for one coach to feed all their thoughts to the other coach who then aligns with his thoughts to deliver clear concise messages and only he speaks. The other co-coach could go around, checking in with individuals and giving them some quiet encouragement (a pat on the back for example).

These roles can clearly be thought out in advance in training sessions with each coach delivering a particular aspect of a session and the other fulfilling a contrasting role perhaps focussing on giving individual feedback for example.

A co-coach also gives you the opportunity to hand over your child into their specific care during a session. They can be responsible for delivering any feedback, encouragement and words of support to your child whilst remaining objective.

They can also be invaluable in keeping you as objective as possible. Ask them to watch you in your sessions and ask for feedback both in your coaching and how you are handling some of the relationships in the group?

They can help you to be consistent with your selections, ensuring that you are picking the right players for the right reasons and not allowing your own emotional attachments to help influence some of your decisions.

You need someone to hold you to account in the right way at the right time. Your relationship with a co-coach will grow and you will learn together but the key is that you trust them, have clearly defined strategies and roles. Get this right and you will have a wonderful relationship working together.

Have a clearly defined game time and selection policy

Some of the biggest angst caused for other parents is based around game time and selection policy. Now we are not here to tell you how to do this but certainly at a young age we recommend that every child is getting equal playing time and that you rotate fairly your selections on a weekly basis.

However, if you go away from this then you must communicate verbally and in writing to all parents and players how you will be selecting the teams and what the criteria is. On paper this can be the easiest thing possible, however, when competition kicks in and you feel under pressure to achieve results, this can go out of the window.

It is this uncertainty and element of surprise that can often cause friction amongst the parent group.

It has been great in recent times to see sporting organisations take the heat out of this situation for coaches such as England Rugby who introduced the 'half game rule' for all children involved in the squad on matchday.

Be proactive with this so that everyone understands the process before the season gets underway, be consistent with what you have agreed, despite any external pressures and this will allow people the opportunity to choose if this is going to be the right environment for their child.

Share out the captaincy

In the early years the captaincy role is nothing really more than a novel way of giving children the experience, the opportunity to talk to them about some aspects of leadership and let them enjoy going up for the coin toss at the beginning of the game. The kudos of having the captains arm band is a big moment for any young child.

With the vast majority of work been done by coaches at the younger age group there is no real reason why every child should not be given this opportunity and the role can certainly be shared out. You will immediately remove any potential point of conflict on this front.

As children get older you can go into more detail about the kind of values that you are looking for in a good captain, it most certainly should not be given to the best player which is often the case. Take the time to find out what traits you are looking for in a good captain and communicate those with the group. Perhaps the role can continue to be shared out but between less players.

By the time children hit the teenage years you can start to see the real leaders stand out and at this stage the captaincy role can be done purely on merit.

It would be an extremely bold move to make your own child captain of the group that you coach, unless they are such an outstanding candidate that no one would have any issue with that. If this is not the case, you may well be opening up yourself and your own child to behind the back comments and criticism.

Share out the numbers

In team games, certain numbered playing shirts can be favourites of the children, often based on some of the heroes they watch on TV. In youth football, numbers 7 and 10 can be popular as children would like to be Ronaldo or Messi. Very few will naturally gravitate towards the number 2 jersey. If you are a coach of younger players, be conscious of this and share the shirts around.

Have a Substitution Policy

Try to ensure that you operate some kind of rotation policy. Picking the same starting team each week and having the same substitute can cause some problems and is probably best avoided.

Be wary of weekly awards and end of season awards

We all like to reward our children with some form of recognition and sport certainly provides a platform to do this. However, I suggest that coaches think really carefully about weekly awards and the end of season bash.

Having awards for man of the match, player of the year or top goal scorer all tend to be awarded to the same players on a regular basis and leaves some players with very little opportunity to be recognised.

This can cause some friction amongst other parents and can leave some children feeling undervalued particularly if your own child scoops these awards.

That does not mean to say your child cannot get deserved recognition but perhaps allow the co-coach to give out the awards, or even involve the parents in the process and have a mini vote.

Think about the type of award that you are giving out as can you reward other things such as commitment, the most improved, the player with the best attitude, the highlight of the game, the best teammate and the best sportsmanship.

These are just a few suggestions but focussing on key processes that make it a level playing field for all players, are more likely to create a greater harmony amongst the group, whilst also show what we should be really valuing during a young players sporting experience. There is also the award chosen by the players themselves, this one often meaning more as it's picked by their peers.

" *Trying to balance out fairness of my own child with how it is perceived by others is a constant challenge and even though I do my best I am still not convinced that this is how everyone else sees it."*

SECTION 2 – COMMUNICATION WITH PARENTS

Have a clear communication policy

Your communication policy should be proactive, consistent and should be a two-way process.

On a basic level you will need to communicate weekly logistics around training and meet times as well as kit requirements and any other pieces of information that you need to share.

This can be done via email, text, social media or a WhatsApp group but I would encourage you to look at some of the options available on the market, with apps like Spond. These will allow you to manage everything to communicate with your group in a safe and secure way and provide a better platform for you to help stay on top of all aspects of running your team, including the financial aspect.

Proactive communication from a coach is vital, especially for mitigating surprises that arise during the season. Parents struggle with the element of the unexpected when it comes to their child. If you can be honest, up front at all times, and communicate effectively before an issue arises, whilst parents may not like the news, they will have time to take it on board, reflect, and perhaps even prepare their child.

In addition, proactive communication will prevent those small misunderstandings from developing into full on side-line issues mid-season. Parents want to know what is happening.

Schools use newsletters to help parents stay informed, support the learning process at home, and be armed with knowledge when speaking with their child.

Coaches should do the same, so parents know why you do what you do, so they can support what you do at home, and they can be guided in how they talk with their children.

Likewise, it does not have to be bad news. Parents are often under pressure juggling their own life commitments. The more information you provide, the better prepared they are for schedule changes, unexpected events, and the like.

There may come times when you have to make late changes or you get in a muddle with your admin, all coaches will tell you that we have all done that from time to time. Having a policy of being proactive and upfront at least creates some good will during those times of difficulty.

Parents have both the right and the responsibility to inquire about all activities that their children are involved in, including sports. For this reason, coaches should be willing to answer questions and remain open to listen to parents' input.

Remember that communication is a two-way street. If coaches keep the lines of communication open, they will be more likely to have constructive relationships with parents. Many times, parents want to be heard and they can provide vital clues to their child and background that can make a coach's job easier. You have to be accessible within a structured communication framework.

Face to face communication is vital. In this technological day and age, it is so easy to blast out an e-mail and leave it at that. Your eye contact, body language and voice tone will tell parents just how confident you are in what you believe is the right way to develop their children.

This also provides you with the ability to read the full spectrum of their communication channels, and therefore develop good rapport. Text and email do not convey meaning and emotion properly. Face to face allows you to match moods, it is easier to persuade or educate someone with eye contact, and misinterpretations are kept to a minimum.

Done right, face to face communication can inspire greater confidence in parents.

Fostering two-way communication does not mean that parents are free to be disrespectful toward coaches in word or action. Rather, it is an open invitation for parents to express their genuine concerns with the assurance that they will be heard by the coach. There is, however, a proper time and place for parent-coach interaction. This goes back to setting agreed upon standards with parents.

You should not be been bombarded at anti-social hours or on a Sunday evening whilst spending time with your own family, but these guidelines need to be set out and agreed upon in advance.

That time is not during practice or a game, and it is never in the presence of the youngsters, unless this is invited by the coach who feels that the three parties being together will provide the greatest outcomes.

You should tell parents what times and places are best suited for discussions, and how to best communicate certain topics. Text will suffice for some, but face to face must be used for more sensitive and personal discussions.

No matter what you do or communicate, sometimes parents will disagree with what you are doing. Try not to get too defensive, although I appreciate that this can be difficult.

You need to listen to what the parents have to say. You might find some parents' suggestions helpful. However, even if you do not agree, you can at least listen and evaluate the message.

Parents simply want to be heard and want to feel they have a say in how other adults interact with their child. Most parents, after voicing their concerns, discover they feel better having interacted with someone who was willing to listen and trust that person more.

Coaches, you will get the final say in the end, but listening can provide unknown insights, provide context, and disarm a potential conflict. Finally, remember that no coach can please everyone.

" *I feel sometimes that it is no longer about just coaching that I need to think about but also proving to other parents that my child is not getting preferential treatment."*

This is one of the most valuable uses of time. Parents time is incredibly precious so try to run a meeting when they would already be at the club, perhaps whilst their children are training with other coaches. You do not have to panic that you are responsible for all of this and if you are uncomfortable with speaking in public, there should be plenty of senior people within your club who are able to facilitate this.

It is important to note here that we do not lecture parents in any of our material as our way of doing things – we believe that this leads to the 'us vs. them' tag. You should focus on informing and supporting the sporting journey – a subtle change in language, but in talking to parents, you need to understand that they are fed up with being preached at and, quite frankly, adults do not like to be told what to do when it comes to the parenting and support of their own children.

Parents will want to be a part of positive cultural standards that are set by the coach *and* parents during a pre-season meeting.

Agreed upon philosophies, behaviours, values, and vision go a long way to creating collaboration. Switching the tone from telling them how to behave to "shared standards" creates more buy-in.

If you do not set the tone, parents will develop their own culture and that may not support your goals. For example, if you are all about winning, shouting at officials and joystick coaching, you should not be surprised to learn that the parents will follow suit. Setting the standard ahead of time saves coaches a lot of headache, heartache, and maintenance during season.

Successful coaches are aware of the importance of securing the aid and support of well-informed parents. Rather than facing the task of dealing with problem parents, a pre-season meeting is the key to reducing the chances of unpleasant experiences.

In other words, having a coach-parent meeting is well worth the additional time and effort, for you, the parents, and the athletes!

Here is a template for a standard parents meeting:

Welcome and Introductions

Coach's background as athlete, coach, parent, etc. Let them get to know you. It is much easier to create allies if they see you as a person first and coach second.

Coaching Philosophy

Ask for parents' support in building a team culture that will reinforce those principles you, the club, and the players hold dearly. Your philosophy will become a guide for how they view and interact with you. Knowing it ahead of time will help parents navigate their interactions with you and support your work with their children.

Team Standards and Expectations

This can be handled several ways. You can set the standards and seek agreement from everyone, you can share outlines of standards and seek input to come to agreement on what matters, or you can work with parents to develop the standards during the meeting. All three contain an element of engagement and empowerment, which is vital to parent buy-in and support.

- Hand out any codes of conduct, possible team values, etc.
- Style of play, instruction from the side-line, training standards, and off-field procedures during matches and tournaments
- Playing time, starting line-ups, captain selection
- Missed training sessions, late arrivals, and more
- Parents involved in debrief at end of training and matches

- Communication lines — how you will contact them, method, consistency and when best to contact you (time of day).
- Parent roles — come with a list of possible roles parents can play and use "can we get a volunteer?" The more roles and tasks you can ask parents to fill the more engaged and supportive they will be and the easier your life will be.

Example parent roles:
- Team photographer
- Social coordinator
- Team admin
- Team Accountant
- Assistant Coach

Logistics

Training Times, Match day, Kit, Equipment, Match Times, Meets, Phone Numbers, Addresses, any changes — coach to be as proactive as possible.

Regular communication schedule — how and when will you communicate and what will be the content of these communications.

How we are partnering in the development of their children

Assure them part of your role is to be a partner in developing their child for success beyond the game, and this requires collaboration and communication to do so. We need to work together for the betterment of the children.

Try to schedule a couple of parents meeting throughout the season to update, see where we are, and keep the lines of communication open.

Dealing with a disagreement — policy

Always have a cooling off period after a game/training or after the incident, at least 24 hours. Emotions can be high straight after a game and is probably not the best time to enter into serious dialogue.

Set a procedure for how to address disagreements. Remind them you have a family too. Be clear on what do's and don'ts for the conversations are. Setting the standards and procedures ahead of time saves a lot of problems later on.

Get to know your parents

If you want them to respect your profession, respect theirs and tap into what they have to offer. Some parents have job-related, or life skills that can be of use to the club. Employ those skills and engage them in their domain of expertise.

Goals and hopes for the season

Coaches goals and hopes & Parents' goals and hopes.

Ask Parents for their opinion? What skills would they like to see their child develop? What is most important to them about the whole experience? Use questions to steer them towards positive character traits and processes as opposed to outcomes and winning.

This meeting must be a two-way process with plenty of opportunities for parents to talk through activity and questioning. Research shows that the best engagement with and best learning of material happens in situations that employ interaction and application. Do not simply lecture but create an interactive meeting that requires participation.

Also, in creating an open atmosphere for exchange, it is very important to show respect for the parents. They should feel that they are a contributing part of the meeting, rather than a mere audience.

Thank you

Finally, at the end of the meeting, you should thank the parents again for attending. You need to be aware of the fact they are also putting a lot of time and energy into the sports experience, perhaps not as much as you.

Hopefully, they will thank you on a regular basis as well for the time that you give up.

If possible, it is highly desirable to schedule a mid-season meeting with parents. This will provide an opportunity to present refresher points, discuss the children's progress, and cooperatively seek solutions to existing problems.

A post-season celebration is an excellent way to end the season. This could take the form of a family dinner planned by the parents, a bowling trip or even a paint ball trip. If you do awards, consider doing "values-based" awards as we discussed earlier in the chapter using the values your team established at the pre-season meeting.

Parents then get to see how their involvement led to a positive result, it guides them to be more focused on values/process rather than game outcomes and is a great way to boost a culture for the following season.

As you become more confident in delivering parents meetings and engaging with your parents, you may want to consider being more creative.

Try playing some games with your parents and consider having an open forum where they are able to ask the questions.

Some of the questions you may not even have considered but in answering them and taking this approach, parents will feel equipped with the information that they really need, not what we think they need.

We discuss this in more detail in our coaches' book 'Engage' which you can find more details about at the back of this book.

You could also ask parents verbally or create a feedback form (google forms are good for this) to give to them so they can point out things that went well and provide suggestions for making improvements next season.

If you can put all of these things in place, then it should allow you to focus on the main reason that you got into the role itself and that is coaching your own child and the rest of the group. You want to be able to invest as much energy into this as you can without unwelcome distractions.

This may all look daunting, but it is better to be ahead of the game with this and have the time to reflect and think about your strategy, rather than reacting as you go along, which can inevitably lead to further issues.

- Consider if a co-coach will work well for you?
- Have a very clear communication policy
- Have clearly defined reasons for all that you do and be prepared to explain them (e.g. team selection, game time, awards)

As a coach consider:

- Running a parent meeting and provide regular opportunities for parents to give you some feedback
- Allocating other roles to parents to help assist you (fundraising, photographer, social co-ordinator)
- How you are going to deal with any disagreements/conflict?

As a parent consider:

- Asking the co-coach or another parent to take on the role of parent of your child whilst you are coaching the team
- Whilst being fair, not talk too much about your own child and their performances and achievements
- How you would like it to look if you were a parent on the other side of the fence?

It has allowed us to share a set of values and interests together. I am really conscious of trying to be a good role model and the sporting experience has allowed me to share some of the values I believe in in a positive environment."

CHAPTER 6
Managing "Pre Match Conversations" With Your Child

The journey to and from the match will provide an interesting dynamic for you both. You will be thinking about the game and what you need to do before hand and afterwards with your 'coaches hat' on but you are still technically a parent as well. You will probably want to analyse and reflect on your performance and your child's performance in the car on the way home.

However, when we talk to parents about managing their child's sporting experience there are probably better times to be doing this. It is sometimes difficult to shut off as a coach and my own experience of coaching tells me this, but perhaps you need to try and keep your own feelings and thoughts to yourself and allow your child to continue to be just that, a child. This is easier said than done.

But how can this impact your child and their performance? Well there may be a danger that you are more excited and fired up than your child and all the sound bites at home and in the car are geared up to 'a big game today', 'are you fired up', "I am expecting a big performance from you today.'

Is it really a big match? To your child it is a normal sporting game and they may see it very differently to you. We know children probably do not view games as big matches unless adults share that information with them.

Your child will naturally be nervous on game day, desperate to do well, desperate to please you as their parent and desperate to make you as their coach happy.

If you are not careful your child will only see winning as a way to satisfy your demands to gain your approval and respect.

Some children are perfectionists to start with and are very aware of their fails and successes.

You must try to avoid adding to this stress.

Many of us will already have been involved in pre-game conversations that may have looked something like this:

"Have you got your kit? Have you got your boots and jumper?"

"I was just thinking last week in training you should have marked the front post at the corner and not the man."

"Also when you had the ball at the back you should have been looking to switch the play, have a think about that today."

"Just remember how good their striker is, try not to give him too much space"

"I hope your goalkeeper plays well today; we could do with him having a good game"

Any advice on how to perform better from you in the car is adding stress to your child's situation.

As our own nerves kick in we often feel like we need to fill in the silence as parents.

Children pick up on their parent's body language and moods incredibly perceptibly. If you are behaving differently to normal your child will pick up on it. Are you quiet and nervous? If so, they may start feeling the same way!

Are you loud and chatty? Another sign that you may be nervous and being slightly over the top and they will also pick up on it.

You have an important role as a parent coach to try and keep your behaviours consistent as well as our body language.

Don't get me wrong, some stress is great for your child. It can help them prepare themselves to do their best. As their stress rises, they may increase their capacity to take on the challenge, meet it with increased alertness, focus and strength. However, there is a tipping point and you need to be aware of this when the stress becomes a hindrance to a good performance.

Try to ensure the car journey behaviour is as normal as possible, just as it would be when going out to the cinema and remember that the ultimate reason that the children play is for fun. Think about taking on the role of DJ in the car and take it in turn to play your favourite music. In my own experience I head towards ABBA as my choice, before been bombarded with some strange rap music which quite frankly I am not cool enough to enjoy when my children take over!

There is plenty of evidence to suggest that if you want your child to put in a big performance you may want to leave them to it on the way to the game.

- Find a routine that works well for you and your children in your context
- Be aware that the car journey to and from matches can be a potential danger area
- - Try to be your usual self, children pick up on changes in behaviour

As a coach consider:
- Not discussing the match/event until you get out of the car
- Not conveying your own nerves and feelings onto your own child
- Using the time to think through your role for the day

As a parent consider:
- Your children will be desperate to please you as dad and coach
- Ask your child — what they would like on the car journey to the game? It could be silence, conversation, music or all of them. Just ensure that you are aware.
- Your own children will have their own nerves and anxieties and need to know that you are there as their parent

" *I feel like I can do stuff to help them which certainly make me feel better about my own parenting. At times it can be tough but this gives me an avenue to feel like I am really helping them.*"

CHAPTER 7
The Car Journey Home

Your game has finished, emotions may have run high, win or lose you and your child may be fatigued, emotional and ready to go home. All of these things thrown into the mix would suggest that is not a good time to have a productive conversation.

However, experience tells us that parents and parent coaches find it difficult to resist these conversations.

Every week up and down the country the car journey home has now extended to the walk back to the car, the car journey home and the return back to the house, a failure of many parent coaches to remove the 'coaches' hat.'

Conversations, sometimes still in the earshot of other parents often follow games along the lines of:

"Why did you do that there?" "Do you remember when you got the ball off the goalie, why didn't you pass it down the wing?" "Why didn't you mark properly at the corner?"

These are examples in a footballing context, but you get the idea and I am sure we have all heard conversations like this.

Most of the time, all the child is doing is looking down or drinking their water pretending to really listen, when actually they probably wish the ground would swallow them up.

The car ride home is when the child just wants to quietly let the game sink in — whether a win or a loss.

Your child will know if they've played well or badly. You don't need to tell them.

It won't be easy for you in your dual roles, but we must remember that the sole reason that our children play sport and will stay involved in sports is fun.

Children want you to be a parent when they finish playing not their coach. Get your 'coaches' hat' off as quickly as possible and certainly it should be gone by the time you get back into the car.

Try to greet your child with something consistent and positive regardless of the result and one of the best pieces of advice we can give here, is to try and treat the highs and lows that you have together in equal measure.

In an ideal world we would let our children lead any conversations in this period after a game, but this can be easier said than done.

We know that lots of parents really value the quality time that they have in the car with their children and often some of their best conversations can happen there, as their children are free from distractions. So, with your parents' hat on and perhaps if you still feel the need to talk after a game to your child that you could maybe ask them some questions that allow the child to reflect on the game/session that they have just been involved in.

"What were the best bits of the game for you today?" "What did you think you did well?" "Was there anything that you were not happy with?" "What do you think you may need to work on to improve?"

This at least allows you both to have a conversation, allows the conversation to be led by the child and guided by you.

One of the biggest dangers here for 'Parent Coaches' is that in speaking with our child, we start to blame other people around the sporting experience. We may have been upset with the performance and attitude of a number of players and we start to complain about them specifically. We may also look to blame officials and if other parents have got under our skin, we may well criticise them without even realising that we are doing it.

This should be a 'No Go' area. As we mentioned earlier in the book, our children will take their lead from us. In making excuses we can make that acceptable for our children to offer plenty, which they will if given the opportunity, but it also potentially weakens our children's relationships with other players and their parents as they start to see people in a different light.

As with the journey to the match, get into a routine for the journey home that works well for you and your family that allows you to manage this time in a healthy and positive way.

I am happy to share with you all that this has been the most difficult time for me as a sports parent and coach during my own children's sporting experience and something that I have had to work really hard at, reflect, tweak and adjust on a regular basis to now be at the point where I am happy with what we do.

However, that does not mean to say there has not been the occasional relapse even with the best well thought out plans.

KEY POINTS

- Speak with your children and have a regular set routine (DJ's on the music works well) regardless of the outcome
- Get rid of the 'Coaches Hat' as soon as you can
- If you are going to ask questions, ask ones that allow your children to reflect on their performance

As a coach consider:
- Your children may not wish to go over the game with you. Is now a good time to talk?
- Use the time to think the game through, calm your emotions so that when you are at home you can settle back into family life
- Don't criticise other parents in front of your own children even if they have upset you,

As a parent consider:
- Do not be in a rush to make any excuses (too much of this and our children follow suit)
- Don't blame officials or other players on the team, this will weaken your children's relationship with them
- That silence is ok – as long as your children know you are there from them (a touch on the shoulder will suffice) they will be fine with it

" *We spend so much time together now, travelling to and from training and matches it can be difficult to know when to give my child time and space."*

CHAPTER 8
Leading Sports Figures Tell Their Stories

We have got together with some of the leading coaches in their field, all who happen to be parent coaches.

We asked them to share their experiences with us in the hope that it would help you to see that even the professionals have the same feelings and come up against the same issues that you might during your time coaching your own child.

We hope that you enjoy reading and learning from their shared experiences.

JACQUILINE AGYEPONG

Jacqueline, a 100 m hurdles champion, represented Great Britain at the 1992 and 1996 Summer Olympics, as well as two outdoor and two indoor World Championships. In addition, she won the silver medal at the 1994 Commonwealth Games.

In what circumstances did you coach your own child?

As a parent and former international athlete sports it gave me a great start and a positive mindset to the role. I always dreamed of my own children taking up sports. As I coached athletics and they would come with me to training, it was a natural move for them to join in.

Not having conflict at the beginning and making my child appreciate the basics and me as a coach, she trained with someone else, then when she was motivated and wanted to learn the skills of the event, only then I allowed her to join my training group.

What were/are the best parts of coaching your own child?

The best bit of coaching her has undoubtedly been seeing her develop as a person and athlete and the bond we both share for the event.

What were / are the biggest challenges?

Separating mother and coach has always been a difficult balancing act for my daughter and I. Finding the balance between is it advice or criticism, is it personal or professional has been tough at times but I would like to think that we have worked through this together and learnt from the experience.

What was/is your relationship like with other parents?

In my case it is very cordial. I have all the support from parents and can talk to them and the athletes both individually and collectively about sessions, schooling, home life and anything else that crops up. I think the relationship is helped as I feel that I understand and coach each child as an individual and this gives the parents the confidence in what I am doing.

If you could do it all again what would you do differently?

I would talk more at home as a coach to my daughter from the start, to understand them more as an athlete. This would have created less confrontation and developed more respect particularly in the early days.

What are your three top tips for parent coaches?

1. Listen and talk to your child to understand their individual needs.
2. From the start teach them the mental aspects of life. The game of life is won and lost in the mind. Try to educate and train mental toughness, positive self-talk and resilience which will help them when the going gets tough.
3. Make it fun and build a friendship community within the group stamping out any negativity straight away.

LEN BUSCH

Len is currently the Head Coach of the Sevenoaks Suns of the WBBL (Women's British Basketball League). He was the WBBL Coach of the Year in 2017, 2018 and 2019 and has led his team to numerous trophies in recent seasons.

He has coached junior female teams since 2005. The Suns Juniors have won 22 national championships in various age groups (U14 to U18) and have sent 26 players to the USA on university scholarships. He has also been involved with Junior National teams since 2009 and is currently the GB U20 Women's Head Coach.

In what circumstances did you coach your own child?

I had been coaching basketball in a NYC High School for a few years when my first daughter was born. My second daughter was born a couple of years later. I remember getting one of those plastic hoops and putting it in the driveway and watching my oldest daughter Kristen make basket after basket. In my ninth year coaching in NY my wife had our third daughter. The next year my wife was offered an opportunity in London. She was a very successful investment banker and we decided to make the move.

I saw it as a great opportunity to spend a lot of time with my kids. The coaching job I gave up was a good one, but I never saw myself coaching HS basketball for 30 years and as I started coaching quite late and had a young family, I saw the college coaching path as a nonstarter.

After a couple of years in London, I started a local basketball club for youngsters so that I would have somewhere to take my daughters. It got them a couple of hours on the court and got them used to the basketball world. We entered a team for the borough in the local youth games and I got to coach my two eldest daughters in this competition. I believe they were 10 and 12.

My eldest then moved to a new school and joined the basketball team there. I watched for one year and was unhappy with the coaching she was getting, so I approached the school and offered my help. I coached at this school for the next 12 years and coached all three of my daughters until the youngest graduated at 18. They each became very good players and I enjoyed coaching them.

I also got involved coaching county teams. I was looking for more basketball opportunities for my eldest, when someone told me there was a Bulgarian lady, training girls in Tonbridge Wells. I brought my daughter along and started helping out with the sessions and soon was running the sessions. These were some of the best players from the area and they were from a number of different clubs. This lady had taken them to France to play and they were beaten quite easily. The players and parents asked for more and better training and these sessions were the answer. A year later this group was formed into the Sevenoaks Suns Basketball Club. I volunteered to coach the U18 group. Over the next 15 years I would coach all of my kids at Sevenoaks. The club was very successful winning numerous national championships.

My middle daughter was good enough to play for England and GB national teams multiple times. I was an assistant coach for the two years that she played England U16s. For the past 3 ½ years she has played for the professional women's team at Sevenoaks that has been the most successful team during that stretch. I coach that team as well.

I remember a pivotal moment when I was England U16 assistant coach and my daughter was a year young and fighting to make the team. The head coach picked a player ahead of my daughter, who in my opinion was nowhere near as good as my daughter. I felt that I couldn't advocate for her because she was my daughter. I don't know if it would have made any difference, but it felt difficult. When she failed to make the team, my daughter was quite upset. I remember telling her she had two choices: quit or get to work and get better. I also told her (as I've told many other players) when trialling for a team try not to be number 11 or 12 of the team. In those choices head coaches can pick anyone they want and for many different reasons. It's a prerogative of the job.

I also had the pleasure of coaching with my daughter last summer as I was the Head Coach of the GB U18 Women's team and she was an Assistant Coach. I was very lucky to have her. She works really hard, understands the players and was a hard worker. The situation only arose because the program was put together last minute, and she was the most qualified for the position. The following year, the powers that be thought that she should be put with a different team to broaden her experience with head coaches.

I have been coaching at least one of my daughters for 21 of the last 22 years that I have been coaching.

What were the best parts of coaching your own child?

The best part was the time we got to spend together going to and from practices and games. Another highlight would be seeing them grow and succeed on the court and seeing how that has helped them off the court.

What were the biggest challenges?

The challenges are many. One would be getting past the normal reticence of kids to take advice from their parents. We worked hard on separating the coach-parent roles. Sometimes after a practice or a game, my daughter would be upset and when we got home, I would say, "I am now your father. Tell me what that crazy coach did today." That would sometimes help.

Another would be avoiding other players and parent thinking that I was favouring my child. This was almost never an issue as I generally pushed my kids harder than anyone else. A great moment for me was when a player came to me and said I want you to push me as hard as you push your daughter.

I would say that through most of my career I have pushed kids pretty hard. The beautiful thing about coaching your own kids is you get an immediate chance at home after a practice or a game to "repair". Make sure that they know that you love them and if necessary, tell them that you are sorry for anything you did that may have crossed the line. With other kids, I can remember being at home and not being comfortable until the next practice when I see them and can check with them and make sure that they are OK and apologize to them if necessary.

In terms of the favouritism situation I was definitely not Bobby Knight who famously responded to a players accusation that Knight was favouring his son over the other player, *'You might be better than but he's my son and I love him you so you have to be a lot better.'*

What was your relationship like with other parents?

I can remember very few problems with parents regarding me coaching and playing my daughters. I had other issues with parents at various times, but none involving my kids. It was probably made easier by the fact that my daughters always were the hardest workers and often the best players.

If you could do it all again what would you do differently?

I can't think of anything I'd change. I have generally gotten a lot calmer and smarter as I've aged. I suppose if I knew what I know now back then I'd have been an even better coach. But that's hardly helpful to know, is it?

What are your three top tips for parent coaches?

1. How you coach your kid must be related to what they want to get out of playing. My kids were pretty serious and worked really hard. They were quite talented and were clear that they wanted to get better and go as far as they could. As a result, I pushed them and demanded a lot. If the son or daughter of the coach just wants to play to be with their friends and have a good time, then the coach's job is to facilitate that. It's about what the kid wants. You're not there as coach to relive your own glory days.
2. Make sure that you are not doing anything to give any parent of a player the opportunity to accuse you of favouring your kid. It might still happen, but your behaviour as coach should mean that most players and parents see you as impartial.
3. Back to one again. Make sure you know what your kid wants. If it's too early for them to know, then make sure they have fun.

JOHN CONLAN

John Conlan was brought up in a tough part of Dublin, developing a love of sport from an early age and getting involved Athletics, Gaelic Games, Soccer, Kempo and Boxing. John's biggest love was boxing, a passion that he has clearly passed on to his family. After moving to Belfast in the 1980's, fate would have it that one of his new neighbours

was Sean McCafferty, an Olympian from the Tokyo Games in 1964, who encouraged him to become a Coach at his club St John Bosco. John eventually took him up on this when two of his five boys, Jamie and Brendan joined the club, with a third in Michael joining when he became old enough — or almost old enough. Sean would become John's coaching mentor and the club gave John an opportunity to learn his 'coaching trade' with kid's right through to performance boxers. One of John's proudest coaching moments came when the three boys all won Irish titles on the same day.

Having developed his coaching, John's own progression saw him join the Irish Performance Coaching panel, coaching boxers in the lead-in to the Delhi 2010 Commonwealth Games and London 2012 Olympic Games, before leading the Northern Ireland team as Head Coach for the Glasgow 2014 Commonwealth Games. These roles coincided with son Michael's involvement in the Amateur Performance Programme, giving John a unique insight to his journey having coached him from his first involvement in Boxing, right through to the Olympic Games. Before Michael joined older brother Jamie in the professional ranks, father and son were together as coach and athlete as Michael won Commonwealth Games gold in Glasgow. John continues to the current time as a key member of the Irish Boxing Performance Coaching team.

What were the best parts of coaching your own child?

Without a doubt, the best thing about coaching my own children has been sharing in their journeys and the rollercoaster of their boxing careers, in quite literally a ringside seat. I am clear though that it has been 'their journeys' and I have been very conscious of this having with my own behaviours. I have observed other coaches and parents living their own journey or aspirations through their kids and I was determined that that would not be me.

The experience has helped provide an amazing insight and understanding of my own children, including in their lives beyond boxing. Both Jamie and Michael completed trade apprenticeships with me. I was a self-employed tiler, before all three eventually moved into a full-time boxing environment. This created a uniquely flexible situation where me, Jamie and Michael could adapt in a work context to accommodate to boxing commitments.

What were the biggest challenges?

As mentioned already, both Jamie and Michael served as apprentice tilers, meaning that we worked together, trained together and lived together. This created a bubble in which parent/coach and son/athlete were together all of the time. At times this made it difficult to separate the inevitable frictions from work, training or the home that every set of colleagues, teams and families experience from time to time, and could carry across from one setting to another. The most notable challenge though, was knowing when to push and when not to push. I learnt a lot of lessons on the job about when to consider other factors in their life. This was particular evident with Michael who, after some encouragement from me, took a few months out from boxing during a tough period in his formative years before returning to boxing with more energy and enthusiasm — catapulting himself towards the success he would go on to achieve in the sport.

What was your relationship like with other parents?

Most of my experiences with other parents have generally been positive but I attribute this to the approach I took which was to be the team's coach when coaching the team, not Michael's dad or Michael's coach, but the team's coach. (This is an approach that earned John compliments from his former Head Coach in the Irish programme, in that he never gave Michael preferential treatment, and if anything worked harder in team sessions with the other athletes within the programme.)

This was also helped by a special relationship and level of understanding between Michael and me where things didn't need to be said — they were just known, without being articulated — something as small as a look could be enough to communicate what was required.

When I was giving time to other boxers with full explanations, one or two points would convey the same information to Michael. This removed any possibility of perceptions of favouritism or preferential treatment which neutralised some of the issues that could result from having one of your children within the programme.

If you could do it all again what would you do differently?

Reflecting on the journey I shared as coach with my boys, I would do it all the same again, in exactly the same way. Not because I got everything right all of the time, particularly with Jamie as the first of the boys to take many of the steps, but because every mistake that he did make have helped shaped him to become the person and coach that he is and helped shape who the boys have become. This journey has helped them all to learn and understand what life is all about.

What are your three top tips for parent coaches?

1. First and foremost — you're their parent, enjoy that — be the parent first, coach second.
2. Don't push them to hard, support them — don't destroy the parent relationship over something from the sporting world.
3. Enjoy the journey, it's a great privilege to be in the dressing room to share in the sport adventure with someone who you've raised from a baby — right through to seeing them achieve at the highest levels possible in sport, enjoy the moment, enjoy the process!

EDDIE COPELAND

Eddie is the father of former England international footballer and commonwealth boxing champion Stacey Copeland. A former professional boxer whose career was sadly cut short through injury, he has had an extremely successful coaching career culminating in the highlight of coaching his own daughter, sharing some amazing memories and winning many titles together.

In what circumstances did you coach your own child?

Due to boxing not being allowed for females when my daughter was a child (80s and early 90s) Stacey had taken up football in her schooldays but for many a year she had trained at her grandads boxing gym where I was a coach, she learnt a lot about the art of boxing but not able to compete. Her footballing skills and achievements gained her a foot-balling scholarship in America where she earnt her degree and

captained their football team. On returning to Manchester from America in 2010 she told me she was packing in football and wanted to be a boxer now that it was legal for women to box. My first reaction was that of a parent and being an ex-boxer myself who suffered a career ending eye injury knew first-hand how dangerous boxing can be. My initial feelings were that of a concerned dad, I don't want my little girl to get hurt but it quickly became evident that she would do it with or without me. I made my mind up I'd rather she did it with me than without me and plans were made to get her to competition level from a skill and fitness point of view.

What were the best parts of coaching your own child?

We knew each other's strong and weak points, we had trust which is vital in a one on one sport like boxing. I was also fit enough to spar with her and in the early days I did many nights sparring with Stacey and this was a yardstick that I could use to see her improve. We shared many attributes, competitive, determined, liked to work with a training programme, similar style etc. It was a journey which was shared and the glory and the heartache was shared as it would be with any of the boxers I coached.

The best part for me was being able to share time in a joint pursuit which we both loved and experienced something that was a real exciting journey which is a time that we both cherished and strengthened the bond that we always had, and along the way we made a bit of boxing history to become the first Father and Daughter to win senior Elite titles (formerly ABA titles). It was with pride that I saw her get selected for England and win a European silver medal in her England debut, win 3 ABA titles and get a washing line of medals for England. In 2016 she turned professional and went on to be the first female to win a Commonwealth title to which she currently holds — my time as her coach ended with her turning pro as I could not devote the time required due to family, work and health issues but coaching Stacey was the high point in my coaching career. The coach she picked to train her as a pro Blain Younis is doing a great job with her and trust is evident between them and he has my trust.

What were the biggest challenges?

Fast tracking a 29-year-old athlete who had suffered many injuries to knees and legs from football to a skill set that was suitable to compete. Finding suitable opponents, had to travel a bit in those days (sometimes abroad to tournaments such as the Golden girl in Sweden to get bouts) due to female boxing just starting to develop.

Getting Stacey to rest was a particular issue and this is where trust was important, she knew I was talking from experience, we were both driven people, but not resting (recovery time) at the right time will lead to over training and not being at your best in a contest.

What was your relationship like with other parents?

Excellent, they have to put their trust in me that I will look after their child as if it was my own and because they would often bring their boys and daughters to the gym, they saw first-hand the blood sweat and tears that went into their kids to make them the best they can be and also very importantly that every boxers safety and health was number one priority and I never let a boxer take a beating or get hurt, I would throw the towel in one punch too soon rather than one punch to late and if a parent knows that you have done all you can to train, coach and develop their son or daughter ready for a contest and that they can trust you to look after them during a bout they are on your side. Sometimes parents had to be managed as well as their son or daughter, a critical parent whose own ego gets in the way can be an issue at times.

If you could do it all again what would you do differently?

Absolutely nothing, we worked together on her training plans, her skill sets and getting her sufficient bouts even if it meant travelling the country and abroad. Stacey excelled at her boxing and if there was one thing that would have been in my power to change (it wasn't) it would have been her age. If she was able to box earlier in her life, then she could have been at the 2012 Olympics, but I prefer to look at what we achieved rather than what we didn't. The good and the bad times are all part of life's rich tapestry of experience and Stacey and I shared something that was very special and unique to both of us.

What are your three top tips for parent coaches?

1. Manage expectations you will have strengths, weaknesses and limitations and you need to establish boundaries. This is what is expected when coaching and undertaking training sessions and these are the boundaries for parent/child, discuss with all parties to see if they need to be adjusted from time to time.

2. Turn off the emotional aspect when in the corner or at the touchline and put on your coach's head, you are of no use to them if you are a gibbering wreck or an angry swearing, shouting and obnoxious parent. If it's not going well for your son or daughter, they and the team need your input and knowledge to turn things around even if this means replacing your son/ daughter on the field or pulling them out of the bout. The team and others in the gym want fairness and equal treatment and this builds trust and integrity with the individuals and the team.

3. If you don't have the knowledge and technical ability to coach your children don't hold them back by being precious. Other more experienced coaches or with a different approach can be beneficial, it's all about your child and not you.

JOANNE DAVIS AND JURGEN VAN LEEUWEN

Joanne is an ex professional badminton player who represented Great Britain at the 2000 Sydney Olympics, was a gold and silver medallist at the 1998 Commonwealth Games and is currently a Level 3 coach.

Jurgen van Leeuwen is an ex professional badminton player for the Dutch National Team competing at European events and winning 4 national titles.

They have three children, Ethan is 19 and in the top 8 in the world, daughter Estelle (15) is the Number 1 in Europe and daughter Emilia who is 8 has no interest in badminton.

In what circumstances did you coach your own children?

In both cases our children grew up around the court watching us coach at an academy within David Lloyd called Milton Keynes Badminton Academy. They both started playing when they were nine years old. I would say Ethan was more naturally gifted and Estelle was more of a hard worker.

They would come most evenings and help pick shuttles up for the older players and have a hit with their parents. As mum I coached them more at a younger age, working on fundamentals and as they grew older dad stepped in and took over.

What were the best parts of coaching your own child?

Knowing the sport very well our children were in a privileged position in that we could teach them the grass roots basics correctly which in a lot of young players cases doesn't happen. Seeing their development is very rewarding and having time away from the home environment where you can play sport together is a huge bonus. We have had some good quality sparring as a 4 and it has been a huge and enjoyable advantage. The bond that you develop with your kids by being both parent /coaches is also rewarding as they know that are getting good quality tactical /technical advice from two people that have been through the same processes.

It is also a great feeling watching your child doing something they love and seeing them succeed whether that's perfecting a shot or winning a major event and knowing you have contributed to their goal.

What were the biggest challenges?

Expectation is one of the biggest challenges. We have naturally high expectations and demand the best out of every training session and we are very direct as parents so will say it how we see it, sometimes you need that calming voice at home. I feel that because we are both in the same sporting environment that there is not that person at home that is 'oh well never mind.' We are always demanding the best and if we don't see it we will tell them.

If there has been an issue at home, it is really hard not to bring it to training and vice versa. We had to set a rule that as soon as we stepped in the car on the way to or from training, that the issue was left there and not brought either into the home environment or to training. That has been easier said than done.

Obviously, the ages of the kids are a big factor. When they were younger, they would listen and act on advice given by us but as they got older it was more confrontational as they challenged everything that we told them. This was certainly frustrating for us as parents/coaches.

There have been times when we have been at tournaments with our children and they are blatantly not listening to any advice from us. We have had to get one of the other coaches from our academy to do their breaks as it would have been detrimental to their play and our well-being but at least we were able to recognise this.

What was your relationship like with other parents?

For the most part it has been absolutely fine. Other parents have leaned on us for support and advice as we have obviously played at a high level and know the pathway to be a successful athlete.

Some parents just expect your child to be amazing because of their name and I feel for my kids in that sense, because if they win it's expected but if they lose it's a giant kill.

Over the years it's strange I have become almost like a mother bear who will protect her kids and will challenge unfair treatment from other parents whereas Jurgen is far more chilled out. At one point I had to stop going to tournaments as I found some parents were so delusional about badminton and how good their child was or not as the case might be and I was finding it quite difficult to deal with.

We also have to tread that fine line as we are also coaching our children's competitors in our academy as we are an elite base, this proves a difficult balancing act as we have to be careful that we are not showing favouritism as parents wouldn't trust us and we seem to have navigated that well over the years.

If you could do it all again what would you do differently?

This is a tough question. Both our children learn differently so we adapted with each child. I think sometimes the badminton court and what has happened at a tournament spills over into home life and so naturally as we are heavily involved the kids don't get a break from badminton. I think I would make more of a conscious effort not to talk about work.

We are always looking forward, but it has been a conscious decision not to push our youngest into the game and let her decide to do something else, which is dance, something we know nothing about but can enjoy purely as parents. So maybe we have exhausted ourselves going through junior badminton.

What are your three top tips for parent coaches?

1. Know when it is time to coach your own children and know when to pass them on when the time is right.
2. Be a parent at home and a coach on the court, leave issues in their respective environments.
3. Be aware of how you communicate with your child. We are often harsher on our own children and say things that we wouldn't say to another child we coached.

RORY
DELAP

Rory Delap is a former professional footballer who made over 600 appearances including 360 appearances in the premier league.

He played 11 times for Rep of Ireland and in recent times has become a full-time coach, starting at U14 level and is currently the Stoke City 1st team coach.

In what circumstances did you coach your own child?

I first started coaching my eldest son (Liam) at primary school as a volunteer with some other Dads when he was 5 for 2 years. Then again when he was 15, he was progressing well and ended up training with us when I was coaching the U18's at Derby County.

I did the same with my other son (Finn) who is 2 years younger than Liam for 2 years, again sporadically coaching his age group when his coaches were away.

What were the best parts of coaching your own child?

When they were younger it was great to spend time with them and see them both enjoy playing football, they both showed a talent from young age but I never wanted to permanently be their coach or be seen to be pushing them into football because of my career. Watching them learn from their successes & disappointments, take on challenges and develop over 10/12 years has been great to see.

What were the biggest challenges?

Not being seen as their coach and being sure it was their own choice and not just playing because of their Dad. As above I wanted them to want to be active and play a range of sports which they did but they both showed they were talented at a range of sports, but both never wanted to miss a training session or game. This showed me they loved football.

The biggest challenge for me was instilling my values and beliefs into them which was tough at times, I didn't want to be the parent or coach who plays the game for them and gives them a rocket in the car on the way home.

I tried to not look at their performance/result but couldn't let a lack of effort go!! In Liam's case this wasn't too much of a problem but with Finn it has been more of a slow burner! This being a trait I'd want to see in my kids in all aspects of life not just in sport.

What was your relationship like with other parents?

I'm quite thick skinned but there was a lot of issues around team selection and minutes which we tried to make sure all the lads were very close to the same but is impossible when you have 18 boys. I heard little comments here and there, but I would always speak to the other parents and explain my decisions and give a reason why, which seemed to settle most issues. The most difficult and frustrating thing with other parents was listening to them on the side-line and the anger they have towards their own child, opposition children & parents as well as their child's coach!

If you could do it all again what would you do differently?

I think I got away from coaching them both at the right time/age that I don't think they ever saw me as a coach, with Liam it was difficult as he was coming to the age of a scholar at Derby and I would have had a decision to make about my job as there was no way I would have stayed to coach him at that age.

There were times when things got heated between myself and both the boys over a difference of opinion over their effort and work rate but I'd like to think now they are older they see that this is the bear minimum and has instilled a real competitive edge into them (it has been a nightmare for Monopoly though).

What are your three top tips for parent coaches?

1. Make sure it's their choice, ask them what they think about it. But be prepared if it's a No, don't take it personally!!
2. Try to recognise signs of awkwardness or negative behaviours and step away at the right time.
3. Enjoy it! It's called a game for a reason.

ROSS EMBLETON

Ross Embleton is currently Head Coach at Leyton Orient Football Club.

He has worked for numerous Football Clubs including Tottenham Hotspur, AFC Bournemouth, Norwich and his current club Leyton Orient.

During all of his years working in professional football, he has continued to work with grass roots players including his own son.

In what circumstances did you coach your own child?

I coached my son in 3 different environments, he is a very shy lad and would never want to go to any clubs as a little boy. I originally started an after school club for the reception and nursery kids at his school which got him playing with other kids (he loved football but his lack of confidence around others meant that he had never taken part).

Later, I started a Soccer School of my own for 4-7 year olds which he attended. This has evolved in to progressing the young boys in to a local club, for them to continue to play and do so in teams, I continue to coach him at the Soccer School and now in his team, although to help him progress, another parent manages the team as it is important that he gets to listen to other people than just his Dad.

What were the best parts of coaching your own child?

I wasn't too fussed about him playing football as a baby, I would have chosen cricket or Tennis as a preference. I had little choice though, as soon as he could walk he had a ball at his feet.

The most enjoyable parts of coaching him is obviously seeing him learn new skills and improve but the biggest bonus and enjoyment has seen him develop in his confidence around other children and now seeing him flourish by competing in a team with new friends every weekend.

What were the biggest challenges?

It is very easy for him to ignore me, for us both to be short with one another. I am his Dad so he is used to not taking information on board from me, like his homework etc so this can easily overlap into his football time. Also, since I was his first experience of football coaching, it can now be a struggle to get him to go to or train with other people.

What was your relationship like with other parents?

Very good, we talk about football but on the whole we all have a good relationship. I have loved being a parent again when he plays his matches, I can leave him be, stand back and watch like the rest of them and just support him rather than be involved. It has been eye opening to see how parents and coaches from others team act when you are standing on that side of the pitch.

If you could do it all again what would you do differently?

I don't think I would change much as I did it to get him started and to bring him out of himself and develop his interaction with people, which is improving. He also now has a separate group of friends from those that he goes to school with every day, which is huge for him as he grows up.

If I had to change something, it would be to introduce him to other football or new coaches sooner than we have since he joined his team.

What are your three top tips for parent coaches?

1. Enjoy it, remember why we and the children have taken part in the first place.
2. Be patient, not every child or player wants to be a professional. Create an environment that you and your child loves being part of.
3. Get a balance — give yourself the opportunity to be the coach but make the most of being a parent too, watching from that step back type view can bring just as much reward as coaching.

ADRIAN GRAYSON

Adrian Grayson is the father of former Essex and Yorkshire cricketer Paul Grayson and former premiership footballer Simon Grayson.

During their early years Adrian was heavily involved in coaching both boys as for many years he coached North Yorkshire age group sides in both football and cricket which Simon and Paul were both involved in.

In what circumstances did you coach your own children?

I started informally with them from a very young age like lots of dads in the garden and on the fields. I was fortunate enough to be invited in to coach them when at primary school by the headteacher and I was also head of PE at their secondary school, so I certainly saw a lot of them. Both Simon and Paul played representative football and cricket at U15 level and I was heavily involved with the coaching of them in both of those sports

What were the best parts of coaching your own child?

I loved watching them progress and helping support them to navigate their sporting journeys. I was able to give them dedicated time due to my background in sport and PE and I was very conscious that sport may well open up a lot of avenues for them. I also felt that I was able to be honest and share my own experiences of the sporting journey with them and I would like to think that this helped them, we have always had a very good relationship in that respect.

What were the biggest challenges?

As they progressed and got older it was becoming more important to them and I wanted that success for them as I could see the ability that they had. I was worried that they weren't overly academic and felt that this needed to work out for them, that was an odd feeling as a father.

I was also aware that been from the country how tough it was for them going into environments with city boy's and I had concerns, but they reacted well and learnt to stand on their own two feet.

What was your relationship like with other parents?

In the early years it was perhaps more difficult. I was conscious that there may have been some jealousy towards us as a family. I was also aware that a lot of other parents felt that the boys were only being successful because of my sporting connections and that it put them at a huge advantage. That was not the case but that was certainly the perception.

I like to think though that as time went on, I got on with other parents, certainly in my coaching I tried to be very fair and was always encouraging of all of the players.

I am not one for conflict, so I certainly leaned the art of sitting on the fence and playing mediator where necessary.

If you could do it all again what would you do differently?

Honestly — nothing. Not in an arrogant way but I am so proud of what Simon achieved in his football and Paul with his cricket. More importantly though, I am proud of how they have gone about it and the way the lads are as human beings. They are both very grounded and humble with an internal arrogance that I believe all top sports people need.

I would have been very sad if they had been top performers but not decent people.

Thankfully, things have worked out pretty well.

What are your three top tips for parent coaches?

1. Try to work as hard as you can at being good in your role.
2. Recognise that there will be plenty of ups and downs, but don't get too down on those bad days.
3. Try to be consistent, encourage and be fair to all the players that you coach.

SCOTT DENNY HANN MBE

Scott is an international performance coach, director of coaching at SEGC. He is the head coach at Scottish gymnastics and a mentor to many coaches around the world.

The gymnasts he has worked with have won over 40 medals at European, Commonwealth, World and Olympic level between them — including Max Whitlock who won two Olympic and 3 world titles and an overall tally of 5 Olympic medals. However, his proudest moments are most definitely the relationships created with the athletes he has worked with, but it would be wrong not to mention in 2016 receiving an MBE for services to gymnastics.

In what circumstances did you coach your own child?

As the director at South Essex Gymnastics Club I always have an indirect 'impactful' coaching role. This has always been great as I am not responsible for my daughters training, and it's always only in short bursts of input — where athlete engagement is quite easily achieved. However, during the period of lockdown I have been doing a lot more 'direct coaching' in her training. So, a few hours a day 4 times per week.

What were the best parts of coaching your own child?

In the gym seeing her give her all to achieve what was set is very rewarding.

At home, we both love the sport, and she misses it greatly. Helping her and seeing the gratitude of opportunity to still do some gymnastics is great.

Knowing she wasn't losing too much condition also settled my own concerns as a parent for when we are ready to return.

What were the biggest challenges?

In the gym, it has been ok as I only have a direct impact on her every now and then. At home it has been hard pushing her to do the repetitions and making the transition from dad to coach.

What was your relationship like with other parents?

In my role I am extremely professional with all parents at the gym. However, I have always advised a parent not to be coaching their own child, or to be involved in any way other than supporter and spectator. Not everyone will agree with tis, but I have always felt that this works out for the best.

If you could do it all again what would you do differently?

I have experienced many issues in gymnastics with parents coaching their own children. Some leading to a breakdown in relationship, and others that have led to official intervention. Many years ago, I made the decision that I would avoid this scenario and as a rule our organisation does not permit a parent coaching their own child. However, in recent times during the lockdown I have taken on the role.

The main reasons for it not being a good idea in my opinion is it can affect the parent child relationship; behaviour can be seen as biased by other parents and the role can cloud the decision-making process from a coaching perspective.

Having said that I have seen plenty of success stories, in other sports, but in gymnastics this is rare .

What are your three top tips for parent coaches?

1. Try to gain as much support as you can to ensure you are not doing it alone.
2. Ensure you separate the coaching and parenting — i.e. leave the coaching behind at the gym but equally leave any disputes at home when starting training.
3. Do this as a last resort. It's always better to be a supporter and listener for your child. They need to know that, ultimately, they have you (the parent) to protect them. But if you can't avoid it — communication, mutual respect and athlete buy in is key.

STEVE HARPER

Steve Harper was a professional footballer for 23yrs. He was the longest serving player in Newcastle Utd history (20yrs), making 199 appearances for them including in the Champions League, UEFA Cup and Europa League as well as appearing in the 1999 FA Cup Final. He also played for Hull in the Premier League at the age of 40.

In what circumstances did you coach your own child?

It came about through him playing for an underachieving U10 side. There was one team they couldn't beat, and it was obvious to me how they could beat them. The team in question were far better technically and despite his side being a good team they were tactically poor. I got on well with the coach and halfway through the season asked if I could assist him. We worked well together, and it proved to be very successful 12 months.

What were the best parts of coaching your own child?

The best parts of coaching him was seeing him do well and partly being in control of his game time and development. He was doing very well for the first few years, so it was all ok despite us having some memorable moments.

What were the biggest challenges?

The biggest challenges were trying to differentiate between coach and dad. Trying to treat him the same as everyone else was tough and he almost had to overachieve compared to everyone else. You can be very conscious of not showing any favouritism and he probably suffered for it at times. I remember taking over his team at U13 when their coach quit during pre-season and we went to a tournament in Redcar with 12 players overall. He had arguably been the best player on the day, but I left him out of the starting line-up in the Final 'to keep everyone happy'. I told him I'd put him on at half time which I did and he scored but it was clearly unfair on him as an individual. We also had some spectacular meltdowns from him as an U10/11 where he walked off the pitch and I was in charge of the team so had to ask one of the other parents to go after him.

What was your relationship like with other parents?

I actually found it more of a challenge to manage the parents than the kids. 99% of the time it was absolutely fine as I'm comfortable speaking to anyone, but it forced me to quit on one occasion when a dad confronted me and the mum had 'had a go' at my wife first. This clearly was unacceptable! It was a situation I should've communicated about better as I'd spoken to the youngster prior to the game but not explained it to the parents, it was still unacceptable for me!

If you could do it all again what would you do differently?

At the U10 age group we became successful by coaching them as a team rather than developing them individually. With my current coaching knowledge, I recognise that at such a young age it's about developing them technically as individuals rather than results. The parents actually still talk about them being Champions at U10 (they're now U17!) however we should have done it differently rather than teaching them how to win matches at such a young age.

What are your three top tips for parent coaches?

It can be very difficult to take on this role so I would think very, very carefully before doing it. It's not impossible but it's tough.

1. Be prepared for the difficulties involved and establish with your child that at training/matches you are 'COACH & not Mum or Dad'.
2. Communicate at the outset to all the other parents/coaches that there will be no favouritism and that if they have any issue AT ALL to speak to you directly rather than whisper and go behind the coaches back on the side-lines.
3. Leave the football at the venue! The car journey and home need to be safe havens!

GLEN HARRIS

Glen Harris is currently assistant coach at Manchester United Women's in the FAWSL.

A former Navy PTI and retired Police Officer he has coached for over 25 years, at every level from the grassroots game, through the academy environments and now at the highest level (FAWSL) in the women's game.

In what circumstances did you coach your own child?

I have four children, three daughters and a son. I have coached all of them during their football journey. My eldest daughter was not allowed to play with boys so we started a girls team. She played Junior girls football for two seasons and then at the age of 14 she played in an adult league and continued playing in an adult league for many years, before finally leaving her teaching job to play professionally in the FAWSL. I coached her both as a junior, in the adult league and also in The FAWSL.

My 2 other daughters are twins, both played grass roots football and then girls centre of excellence football, before playing adult football. One went on to play in The FAWSL and the other played for the development side. I coached them both in grass roots football but did not coach them in the centres programme. I did coach the one in The FAWSL (for information there is a 10 year gap between the twins and my eldest.)

My son played one season in grass roots football before entering the boys academy system at 8 through to 18, during that time I coached him twice during his time in the academy system.

What were the best parts of coaching your own child?

The best parts were seeing them develop new friendships, seeing them challenge themselves physically and technically and seeing them learn how to compete, both in a team environment and competing for a place in either a professional team or a centres/academy programme.

I also enjoyed it when they came to me after training or games and we would sit and discuss key learning points and how they could improve their game.

Also how supportive of one another's football journey they were and are. I believe it is part of the reason we are such a close-knit family unit.

What were the biggest challenges?

For me I always found the biggest challenge was not disadvantaging my children by taking the easy option of taking them off, when younger, to give other players playing time. I suppose in a way I was fortunate that I had a 10-year gap and learnt from my initial experience. One example of this was during my eldest second season, we had got to a play-off final, I believe they were U13/14. It was 7-a side league and was playing against our strongest rivals. One of our players for some reason did not arrive in time for kick off. My daughter started the game and at the interval we were leading. The mother and the father of the girl who had arrived late were on at me to get their daughter on. I succumbed and took the easy option and took my daughter off. We ended up losing the game, now I'm not saying if she had stayed on we would've won, but I didn't weigh up other options I just jumped to the easy option.

It was several years later that I found out from my daughter she did not come out of the changing rooms when taken off. This really impacted on me and I believe helped me when coaching my younger children.

What was your relationship like with other parents?

I don't want to sound conceited but I never have had a problem with other parents. I guess I was fortunate that my children are decent footballers and were well respected by both their teammates and parents alike.

I regularly received praise from parents for the way I coached and help develop their children not only as players but also as young people.

I always tried to be fair with all the players but also honest particularly as the children got older and it became more competitive.

One season I created an extra team as we had to many players therefore ensuring players had ample game time. Again this extra commitment was recognised by parents particularly those who realised their child was not at the levels of others.

I recall a parent of one lad, who at the time was one of my son's best friends, I released from the academy. This was one of the most difficult things I have had to do in football. I gave the boy some feedback. At that time his father was not happy with me, however, his son went and played for a grass roots team and I also watched him play in the same school team as my son. It was clear he had improved in confidence. I recommended he came back into the academy programme, which he did and stayed there for the next 3 seasons. His father approached me shortly after he had come back in the programme and thanked me for doing the right thing for his son at the time of his release. He went onto say it did not seem right at the time but in hindsight it was.

If you could do it all again what would you do differently?

I guess the only thing I would do different is to not over-compensate against my own children. All my family have some great memories from being involved in coaching my children in football. They also have some great friendships that they have formed through football.

What are your three top tips for parent coaches?

1. Make sure you create an environment where kids enjoy themselves and want to come back week in week out.
2. Each child is different, work hard in understanding them as individuals and to build a relationship with each and every one of them.
3. Be open and honest with parents keep good lines of communication.

CHRISTINE HARRISON-BLOOMFIELD

Christine Harrison-Bloomfield is a former athlete who represented Great Britain in the 60 m, 100 m, 200 m and 4×100 m.

In her coaching career she has helped coach amongst others Christine Ohuruogu, Anyika Onuora, Andy Turner, Asha Philip, Jodie Williams, Eugene Ayanful and Savannah Williams.

Alongside this she has coached her own children as well as many elite junior athletes.

In what circumstances did you coach your own children?

As a parent and former international athlete, I had a great start in being able to help and support my children in sport. We started at a young age with both children particularly around developing some basic athletic movements in the garden and they used to visit the track with me. In the last five years I have coached them more seriously focussing on their athletic development and their netball.

Initially, I was hesitant about coaching my own children as I did not want to be perceived as the pushy parent but am pleased that I was able to overcome this in my own mind.

What were/are the best parts of coaching your own children?

I have been really pleased that I have been confident in the information I have given them around their technique and the mental support I have been able to provide to help support them during their sporting experience.

They are both very different and my understanding as a teacher and coach allowed me to best support them knowing their own unique set of character traits. I have two daughters, Ella the youngest is outwardly confident and voices her ambitions and what she is going to achieve whilst my eldest Indiya is internally competitive and is great at setting her own goals and aspirations based on what she wants to achieve.

What were / are the biggest challenges?

I had some challenges early on with Ella who is a happy young girl who just wants to have fun and sometimes she overstepped the mark in my training groups. She would often mess around, be cheeky to me in front of athletes and I found that difficult to deal with. It led to several very frank discussions around the importance of attitude.

Both children have been in groups with some very talented athletes and getting them to understand that I would be proud of whatever they achieved as long as they were giving of their best was difficult on occasions.

I think they felt under some pressure not from me but in thinking that they needed to seek my approval by being as successful at athletics as I maybe was. They have now settled on different sports which has perhaps helped this situation.

What was/is your relationship like with other parents?

Over the years there have been challenges. I had one particular group of parents who I felt constantly in conflict with based on what I felt was their aspirations for their own children, rather than that desire coming from the child themselves.

However, I have had many positive relationships with parents, some of whom I would call friends and we have worked together in the best interests of their children.

I make myself accessible to parents but set very clear boundaries about my expectations around the group, ensuring that my athletes are respectful of their parents and the role that they play whilst also ensuring that we are working together on developing the whole individual not just on their child the athlete.

If you could do it all again what would you do differently?

If I am honest, I would not really change anything. However, I am very conscious that my background as a teacher and a coach before I started to coach my children allowed me to recognise some of the things that were going to be important in my role as mum and coach.

What are your three top tips for new parent coaches?

1. Make sure your child/ children love the sport that they are participating in.
2. You have to make sure that they know you love them whatever they achieve with the sport.
3. Support and encourage others even if they beat your child and be honest, making sure your child still feels valued at the same time.

ZAK JONES

Zak Jones is currently the Wales Hockey Senior Men's Head Coach after an illustrious playing career. Zak is a former Welsh hockey international and captained his country gaining 117 caps in the process.

In what circumstances did you coach your own child?

Probably the same as most parents who got involved. We are at a small club and if someone did not coach his team, the boys would not be able to play and so I took the role on as a parent volunteer.

What were the best parts of coaching your own child?

It is just fantastic getting to watch him play and develop every week and to see him enjoying playing the game I am so passionate about.

What were the biggest challenges?

Trying to balance wanting the best for him as a parent and wanting him to do well but also continuing to coach him as I would any other child. In other words, letting him find his own way and not being too hard on him, not letting the frustration of a parent who wants the best for their child to take over.

What was your relationship like with other parents?

I think I am relatively good at compartmentalising being his coach and his dad (most of the time!) and so would like to think that I am fair and open with all the boys and their parents. As a result, I have a very good relationship with the other parents.

If you could do it all again what would you do differently?

I am still currently coaching the U12's and so am still constantly learning and trying to get better at it!!

The biggest thing would be not to be too hard on him. To remove the parent more and coach him as I would any other child and to be really positive with him.

What are your three top tips for parent coaches?

1. Be positive and enthusiastic.
2. Be as fair and consistent as you can.
3. Make sure it is fun and enjoyable for both of you.

GREIG LAIDLAW

Greig Laidlaw is Scotland's second-highest points scorer (714) and has captained the country more times than anyone else (39). A 2017 British & Irish Lion, the Jedburgh-born scrum-half followed in the footsteps of his uncle Roy who starred for the national team in the 1980s.

Laidlaw played three times in Japan at the 2019 Rugby World Cup, where he passed 100 tournament points in Scotland's final match against the hosts.

In what circumstances did you coach your own child?

We were living in a foreign country at the time (France), we are originally from the UK. My son who was 5 at the time joined the local tennis club which he enjoyed but was frustrated with the language barrier, so I started to help out.

This ultimately turned into me coaching him at home. We bought nets and set it up in our garage (a perfect surface for tennis) where I started to coach him on a regular basis.

What were the best parts of coaching your own child?

I guess it's the enjoyment of seeing them improve their skills and the fact they are having fun.

I believe this is the crucial element of kids improving when they are young if they are having fun during their learning/coaching time.

What were the biggest challenges?

It's harder for a parent of a young child to coach them all the time due to the relationship as their attention span of me being "the coach" only lasts so long and they then see me as Dad and rightly so.

What was your relationship like with other parents?

Did not have to worry about this as it was just me and him.

If you could do it all again what would you do differently?

I would probably try and keep it to a set time of day and a set day of the week.

We were pretty sporadic with our timings and this sometimes did not work out as well.

What are your three top tips for parent coaches?

1. Have as much fun as you can.
2. Be patient (ensure you are being the parent as well as the coach at the right times).
3. Be supportive and give loads of encouragement.

STUART LANCASTER

Stuart is best known for being the head coach of the English national rugby union team from 2011 to 2015. Since then he has been a key part of the coaching staff at Leinster Rugby helping them win the Champions Cup in 2018.

Prior to taking on the England role he ran the Leeds RFU Academy for five years from and in 2006 was appointed head coach of Leeds Tykes.

In Lancaster's debut season, he led Leeds to promotion to the premiership with a staggering 122 points.

In what circumstances did you coach your own children?

I coached my son Daniel and daughter Sophie from the age of 5 as they both began playing rugby at West Park Leeds rugby club.

What were the best parts of coaching your own children?

It was great to see them develop not just as players but as people and to be hands on during that process.

What were the biggest challenges?

I guess because I was already a coach my kids never really thought anything of it, in fact I don't think other players or parents thought so either. Both children quickly understood there was Dad (the coach) and just Dad, so we talked about the differences and I always worked to keep the appropriate distance as Dad (the coach!)

What was your relationship like with other parents?

Good, again, I think they all just wanted to learn so I made sure I helped when I could... I was never the Lead Coach; I just supported the lead coaches from behind trying to help and guide them in the right direction.

If you could do it all again what would you do differently?

Not much really, I did parent workshops, coaching workshops and player workshops... we went on tour and again just making sure you are at the appropriate distance from your children, not too close and not too distant as it is unfair on them if you are.

What are your three top tips for parent coaches?

1. Make sure your child understands your role but just be yourself.
2. Don't treat your child any differently than anyone else.
3. Enjoy it, it is a great time to connect and do things together... it bonds you closer if done right in my opinion!

DAVID
LEADBETTER

David is one of the world's leading golf coaches for tour professionals and other golf coaches who go on to teach his methods.

He has had a glittering career and coached Nick Faldo, Greg Norman, Ernie Els, Nick Price, Charles Howell III, Michelle Wie, Lydia Ko and Byeong Hun An.

In what circumstances did you coach your own child?

I taught all my kids from a very young age up until the age they wouldn't really listen to me! My sons started very young, but my daughter only started when she was 12, but was a good listener.

When they got to a certain age, I handed them over to one of our coaches and I filtered information to their coaches, unknowingly to the kids. There were less arguments and rolling of eyes that way. As they progressed, they listened to me a little more after their friends told them that I knew what I was talking about.

What were the best parts of coaching your own children?

Best part of coaching my own kids was that, apart from family holidays I was able to spend quality time with them on the tee, course and at tournaments sharing in their experiences along the way.

What were the biggest challenges?

The biggest challenges were keeping their spirits up when things went wrong, as they often do in golf. For myself it was trying not to get too emotionally attached to the way they were playing and maintaining a calm head, whether the results were good or bad. As a coach you have to maintain a calm demeanour -maybe the odd fist pump but certainly no cartwheels.

What was your relationship like with other parents?

My relationship was great with other parents on the whole as they respected who I was. Occasionally I would let the parent let them know they were acting like an idiot but never in front of their child which I felt was helping them become a better golf parent. I would never criticise a kid in front of their parents and would only offer advice if the parent asked me.

If you could do it all again what would you do differently?

Our kids were never forced to play and played because they wanted to but from a pressure standpoint it might have been easier to play another sport as a full-time profession.

They did play other sports growing up and they decided to specialise themselves, but it was difficult having such a close affiliation to the game.

What are your three top tips for parent coaches?

1. Enjoy the experience together, have fun and make it all about them. In all likelihood they won't be a Tiger Woods or Michelle Wie but golf in particular is a game they can play for a lifetime and which teaches them many life skills.
2. Coach, cheerlead and guide, don't necessarily try to teach them unless you are qualified to do so.
3. When they get to a certain stage and they are keen to progress, hand them over to a qualified coach and let them do their job without interference. Support from afar!

LIZ MCCOLGAN

Liz McColgan is one of Britain's all-time great athletes. During her athletics career she was an Olympic 10,000m Silver medallist and a world 10,000m Gold medallist.

Liz won double Commonwealth 10,000m gold medals and was a 3,000m bronze medallist.

Following her career on the track she went on to win the London, Tokyo and New York marathons.

She has since embarked on a successful coaching career which includes coaching her own daughter Eilish.

In what circumstances did you coach your own child?

My daughter Eilish started running from 12 years old mainly through the school, then joined my local club with a friend. At the time it was really only parents coaching there. I knew from a very early age Eilish had the ability to run well, but in my career, I had seen so many pushy parents that I decided very early on, I would never make her feel she had to run, she had to want to run for herself just like I did. So Eilish never came to my training and very rarely to races as I kept them separate.

In saying that, because I knew she could run I played running games in my garden with her when she was young, we had a 400m loop which she ran on, but it was all fun. I encouraged her to participate in lots of sports so she was active and could find something that she really liked to do.

Then as she fell into running at school and loved it, I said to her stick at it for a year and I will start coaching you, which she did. It was actually only around 6 months when I started to coach her, then built up a group of youngsters, several of whom became national champions, so she had some talented runners to train with.

What were the best parts of coaching your own child?

The best part of coaching your child is you are both on the same wavelength mentally, because it's your child you know them closer than any other athlete.

I suppose control also, you know what their eating, sleeping and daily routine is like, so you can be more honest, caring, direct, as you have that family bond. Also emotionally there is a strong tie. There is a downside though which is protection, it hits you harder if say they get injured or they have a disappointment of not reaching their goals, because you feel the need to protect and take away their pain, as a mother that's a natural instinct.

What were the biggest challenges?

The biggest challenge is not letting family feeling cross over into your coaching. Like persuading you to change your path of your program or ethos. Kids look a lot at what others do and can be so easily persuaded by performances of others, especially when things are not going well. When Eilish was running she would get beaten by girls she used to beat and come home crying *"Oh they're running 10 mile runs, I only run 5, that's why they're better"* I think it's really important for a parent to explain their plans to their children so that they understand where it is going and what the end goal is. To be honest Eilish has been a great learning experience for me as a coach, as she had so many issues growing up that it forced me as a coach to think outside the box for her to progressing her athletics.

What was your relationship like with other parents?

I had a pretty good experience with the parents as I was very honest and upfront and if I felt they were pressuring their kids, I would tell them to back off, as I would push them when they needed to be pushed. I actually would meet with the parents before I started to coach their child and tell them how I worked and how best they could support their child, so it worked pretty well.

I always involved any decisions with the kids and parents so there was always transparency.

If you could do it all again what would you do differently?

It is like everything, things have moved on, I have learned more over the years, so I would not change anything. I would just encompass all my new thoughts and processes into my programs. In the case of Eilish I would never have let her steeplechase but that again was her choice at the time, so I supported her as she loved the event. However, the injury she got while hurdling was career threatening and technically, she was not sound enough.

What are your three top tips for parent coaches?

1. Support your child, let them make the decisions and do not force them.
2. Let them make mistakes but be there to pick up the pieces.
3. Never stifle their dreams.

RACHAEL MACKENZIE

Rachael Mackenzie is a Thai-Boxing champion. Having only started Thai-Boxing in 2000, her hard work and determination paid off when, in 2006, she topped the Women's Thai-boxing world rankings in 2 weight categories (50kg and 52kg). Swapping to boxing in 2016, Rachael won the British boxing championships and a place on the England boxing team. The mum of twins is a Chartered Physiotherapist and CrossFit coach.

In what circumstances did you coach your own child?

I coach my children (11-year-old boy/girl twins) across a number of environments. I set up a CrossFit Kids programme in order to give them the opportunity to train and compete in both CrossFit and Weightlifting. In addition to this as a "sporty" parent I have acquired the role of supporting coaching them across a number of sports. Their primary sport, supported by me is hockey (though I have also coached at rugby, football and cricket).

What were the best parts of coaching your own child?

Having the opportunity to see them develop and improve not just as an athlete but also as a sports leader. As I'm the coach, this seems to give them permission to put themselves forward to lead demonstrations in ways that they don't do in sports I don't coach. Coaching also gives me the chance to have an honest appraisal of their level of commitment to the sports.

What were the biggest challenges?

Not being too critical of them and not transferring my natural competitiveness into them. Whereas I would want to "win" at every training session sometimes they just want to have fun with their friends, and can I find this frustrating.

What was your relationship like with other parents?

Most parents were very supportive however some can be critical and too pushy. On a number of occasions, I've offered the whistle to parents who have been upset with my insistence that in the junior game all children are given an equal opportunity to play and compete.

I found this easier to manage because I applied the same rules to my own children, so they were not given preferential treatment over less able players.

If you could do it all again what would you do differently?

I think learning as a coach and parent is part of the journey. I own my mistakes with my children and that's a really valuable lesson for them. You don't have to get it right all of the time.

What are your three top tips for parent coaches?

1. Realise that, regardless of talent or their perceived level of ability, you are not in control of their success. They must decide their own path.
2. Focus on enjoyment and performance rather than outcome. When you are also the coach, especially with a competitive nature, being aware of your reaction to winning and losing is really important. Reacting in the same way and focusing on those aspects builds more resilient athletes but also builds a more harmonious relationship with your own children.
3. Be more empathetic to varying level of effort. Not every child has the reserves to give 100% in every session. Recognising this and asking the question "how are you feeling today" a bit more often would have saved some of the frustration I encountered.

PATRICK MILEY

Patrick Miley was originally a Civilian Helicopter Pilot working for Bristol Helicopters on the North Sea.

He developed the Aquapacer Electronic Programmable Swimming Training system 1991-2003 and enjoyed working with many Olympic Medallists from around the world including Paul Palmer, Ian Thorpe, Brooke Bennet and Misty Hyman. One in every 3 Olympic Gold Medallists from Sydney 2000 Olympics were using the system.

He was the Head Coach at Garioch ASC from 1990-2016 and is currently the High-Performance Swimming Coach at the University of Aberdeen.

He was also a coach on many Great Britain and Scottish International Teams at the following events: European Junior Championships 2005, European Short Course Championships 2005 & 2008, European Long Course (LC) 2006, Olympic Games 2008 & 2012, World LC Championships 2009, 2011, 2013, Commonwealth Games 2010.

In what circumstances did you coach your own child?

It has been a really unique journey as we introduced Hannah to the pool at the age of 3 and she was swimming within a club environment at 5. I was the club coach at the time, and I have been involved from that point on throughout her whole swimming career at both junior level and as a senior athlete, taking in numerous Olympic and Commonwealth Games and World and European Championships.

What were the best parts of coaching your own child?

I loved watching the progress that she made and her evolution into a world class swimmer, considering how physically small she has often been in comparison to other swimmers.

I took great pride in seeing her dedication to the sport and admired at a close distance how she managed to schedule herself and dedicate time to her academic studies and her training.

She was always comfortable with being different to her peers, particularly during those teenage years, when her school colleagues didn't really understand her life choices and would encourage her away from the path that she was taking.

I really respected that and started to see that she had a really steely determination that I had maybe doubted in the earlier days.

I also felt that I had a unique insight into Hannah the person, I knew so much more about her behaviours and if there were any other issues being carried over from her personal life into her sporting life. I valued that unique part of the relationship.

Most of all she taught me as much as I taught her both in and out of the pool and that is something I will fondly remember.

What were the biggest challenges?

I think the biggest challenges were managing the disappointments, I found this a really tough one. With an Olympic medal being a long-held goal, coming 4th in Rio in 2016 was a tough one to take and having 4 years between Olympic cycles makes it an even harder one to take.

Watching your child work so hard to achieve their specific goals and then come up a fraction short hurts and I am sure that every parent feels that pain in whichever endeavour their children may be taking part in.

What was your relationship like with other parents?

On the whole I like to think it was very positive. I felt that I looked after all of the athletes that I coached and did not show preferential treatment to Hannah particularly in the early days when I was a club swimming coach. I don't remember any huge areas of conflict and I did my best to support parents understanding of performance based on my own experience as a helicopter pilot and my time in the military.

On reflection I do feel that when Hannah outgrew the club environment her performances had taken her comfortably ahead of her peers and I think that helped in other parents wanting her to do well as opposed to seeing her as direct competition to their own child.

As a result of this I hope that most of my relationships have and remain both healthy and positive.

If you could do it all again what would you do differently?

There were times throughout her career when I wished I had been there even more. I have only been in full time coaching for the last few years and before that did my helicopter flying and ran my own business Sometimes I had to coach from afar and you wonder if that was the difference between some success and failure.

However, when I talk and think about this, I often felt that this made her stronger and more independent and might be a key factor in why she is still swimming today and achieved what she achieved.

What are your three top tips for parent coaches?

1. Try to ensure that you do nothing to damage your personal relationship. You must have a personal contract with yourself on how you need to behave and also one with your child where you both understand how it is going to look. This will consistently change as well so be prepared to adapt and tweak it.

2. Make sure that you are enjoying the process.
3. Finally, make sure that the rest of the family feel engaged, are enjoying and supportive of the whole process. My wife has been such a crucial figure and as Hannah describes her, 'the glue that holds it all together.'

PAUL NIXON

Paul Nixon is a former professional cricketer who played for Kent, Leicestershire and England. As a coach he has been the head coach of the Jamaica Tallawahas in the Caribbean Premier League, the head coach of the Chattagram Challengers in the Bangladesh Premier League and is currently Head Coach of Leicestershire County Cricket Club.

In what circumstances did you coach your own child?

Our daughter Isabella has just turned 12 and she loves her netball. Our coaching has very much been centred around the garden where the grass is bare from our activities. We play and practise lots in the garden and we work on mental routines to athletic movement & biomechanics which has led to her having good movement and hand skills. We have had to advance her development as she currently plays in a team a few years above her current age.

What were the best parts of coaching your own child?

The best parts are rolling up our sleeves and having a good laugh together. Knowing our child as well as anybody has really helped us develop a style of coaching and play that is suited to her learning and what motivates her.

My sporting background has allowed us to supplement the other coaching she receives and be really systematic and accurate in our processes.

What were the biggest challenges?

The biggest challenges are getting into Isabella's mind that even though I don't and have never played netball that the movements and type of training are that we use are used in many different sports.

At times it has been difficult to motivate her during a change in her body with hormones kicking in and I have found that tough. It was particularly hard during the Covid 19 outbreak as she wasn't with her friends playing through the week & weekends so didn't have an end goal and focus to build up to. This made motivation extremely tough for her.

We tried to talk about hitting the ground running and when she returned and saying she can only be in control of what she can control – this seemed to help.

What was your relationship like with other parents?

I have not been directly involved with coaching my daughter's teams and I try to keep a distance when watching and supporting and leave the coaches to it.

I do try and keep everyone as positive and happy as I possibly can when I am around the other parents.

If you could do it all again what would you do differently?

I wouldn't really change anything. Having some structure has really helped and just letting fun be the primary goal has certainly worked for us as a family.

What are your three top tips for parent coaches?

1. Make it fun.
2. Get your children to understand their strengths.
3. Get your children to design their own sessions and help you design yours.

CARISSA TOMBS

(nee Dalwood)

Carissa Tombs is a former Australian Netballer who gained 94 caps between 1988 – 1999. As a player she was a member of 3 winning world champion-ship teams and 2 winning commonwealth games teams amongst many other honours. She was later awarded an Order of Australia medal and was inducted into the Australian Hall of Fame.

As a coach she has been a club coach with Collaroy Netball for the past eleven years, coaching in various age groups, a coach with NSWIS Coaching and been involved in coaching the NSW U19 team.

In what circumstances did you coach your own child?

The circumstance is probably the same in many instances, no one else put their hand up! After I retired from International Netball, I had many years off, so the time felt right, to coach my children and to ease back into the sport I love, was a wonderful opportunity.

I have 3 daughters, all of whom I have coached at some point throughout their junior Netball journey and I am currently still involved in coaching my youngest who is 13.

With each of the girls I ensured I had one or two seasons off, I felt it was important that they received input from other coaches, to broaden their Netball knowledge, appreciate new ideas and different coaching styles.

What were the best parts of coaching your own child?

To be involved in your child's sporting development is pretty special, watching them first-hand enjoying every aspect of their chosen sport.

Teaching tolerance, patience, teamwork and working towards common goals so not only my child but other team members are well rounded athletes.

When you work hard each week as a coach to achieve your team and individual goals, it's not only your child that benefits.

I like to see the girls I coach end up being good people on and off the court.

What were the biggest challenges?

The challenge in the early days for me was to not focus too much on the other team members, often if your child is competent it is easy to neglect their needs, getting the balance right is important to all involved.

The other challenge is to create a harmonious team — no one is alike physically or mentally, managing each individual so they all play at their best ability and most importantly as a team unit, it's a constant work in progress and balancing act as you need to harness their different traits without stifling their individualities. To get the balance of Parent/Coach/Athlete right is very rewarding.

What was your relationship like with other parents?

I have always had a great relationship with the parents throughout the years, there has always been unwritten boundaries and mutual respect.

I think the key is to stand away during the game and breaks don't divulge too much information and don't talk out of school.

If you could do it all again what would you do differently?

There really isn't too much I would change — I have enjoyed every aspect of having "two hats".

What are your three top tips for parent coaches?

1. Make the sessions fun — the skill of incorporating fun whilst learning will keep the athletes interested.
2. Have a session plan and keep it structured.

3. Don't favour your own child nor overcompensate by neglecting their needs.

MICHAEL
VAUGHAN

As mentioned at the beginning of the book you have a choice to make about whether it is right for you to coach your own child. I personally felt that it was not right for me and former England cricket Michael Vaughan is yet to take on the role of coaching his own children but hasn't ruled it out for the future.

We spent some time with Michael getting his thoughts and advice on the topic.

I have encouraged all of my children to take part in a wide variety of sports and all the time I keep coming back to the question that is most important to me, as dad; it is - are my children having fun participating?

I have helped out with guidance and advice but have taken a step back from the technical side of coaching preferring, to leave that with the coaches who are directly involved with my children.

I also believe that children need to find their own methods and be given the freedom to express themselves, without being clogged down with too much coaching information. If I added all my technical input to what they are already receiving, then I would be contradicting myself.

I happily hand them over to their coaches and it allows me to be simply one of the dads, which I really enjoy, and I always makes a conscious effort to give the coaches space to do their job, whilst I do mine as a parent.

Whilst I do not provide too much technical input to my 14-year-old son, who is involved in the Cheshire cricket set up, I do use my playing experience to talk him through some situation play based my own experiences.

My experience in sport tells me that the journey needs to be allowed to happen. At no point in my mid-teens did I believe that I was going to be an England cricketer and as a parent, I recognise the importance of viewing sport as a long-term journey and that journey being unique to every individual.

As a parent I get frustrated when the basics have not been taught well across all sports and I believe coaches have a huge responsibility in this, as the children simply do not know.

I feel nervous just like any other sporting parent when watching and I naturally wants all of my children to do well, but when I do talk it through with them, I acknowledges that, particularly in cricket, it is not always going to be their day.

I do worry that on occasions parents want it more than the child, that the child is made out to be better than they actually are and then the child struggles under extreme pressure to perform in environments that they are not equipped to deal with. As long as my children are working hard and enjoying it then there is absolutely no pressure from me and I simply love being dad.

My three top tips for parent coaches:

1. Make sure that they are enjoying playing.
2. On game day – leave them to play, the work has already or should have been done.
3. Try not to overdo technical training – it can lead to the creation of robots and players who are unable to appropriately express themselves.

ANTHONY VIGGARS

Anthony Viggars is the father of Meg Viggars who played for both England junior and senior volleyball teams and represented the UK in Beach Volleyball at the 2008 Youth Olympics in Australia.

In January 2020, Meg captained England women for the first time at the Novotel Cup in Luxemburg.

In what circumstances did you coach your own child?

In late 2006 it was apparent that my 12yr old daughter Meg, who was a very talented all-round athlete, was beginning to favour volleyball over other sports. She trained at my cub Newcastle Staffs amongst a talented group of girls. who clearly needed an experienced coach to help them reach potential. Having been a player/coach at the top level of English volleyball for approximately 16 years at this time and a having a clear vested interest in wanting the best for my daughter, I volunteered for the role whilst initially continuing to coach the club's men's team.

The girls went onto have great success, winning National titles at under 14, 15 and 18 age groups and travelled abroad to play in competitions.

What were the best parts of coaching your own child?

Spending the extra time with her as she was growing up, creating and sharing memories that we will both always remember.

What were the biggest challenges?

Leaving the sport side of our life in the sports hall and just being father and daughter outside, not only for our own good but also for that of other family members. We were both obviously driven sport wise and volleyball was never far from our thoughts.

What was your relationship like with other parents?

I was very lucky indeed with other parents and found them very supportive and had very little conflict. I guess the fact that we were a winning team helped. Several took on roles such as organising transport, booking hotels, buying kit etc all of which meant that I could just solely focus on the coaching side of things. I really did feel that we were all on a journey together. Having witnessed many other coaches (across various sports) in similar situations, I realise that this is far from always the case and will always be grateful for their help.

If you could do it all again what would you do differently?

If I'd known in advance the role that I was going to take I would have begun working with experienced junior coaches in advance, rather than jumping in straight at the deep end.

Whilst being an experienced player and coach of senior men, I was pretty much learning on the job regarding being a coach to juniors. At the time this felt quite a responsibility as the girls were clearly a talented group and I did feel pressure for both the team and individuals, such as Meg, to succeed.

What are your three top tips for parent coaches?

1. Try to leave the game in the gym — not always easy!
2. Whilst you obviously can't show favouritism, your child does though need praise as much as any other player.
3. Remember you're their coach for a short period but their Dad for life.

As you can see from the vast majority of these interviews, there are many differences of opinion, as you would expect across such a range of sports and environments. However, the overriding message is that the experience should remain fun for our children and that all of us involved should be enjoying the experience as much as we possibly can, with our children's happiness at the forefront of our minds.

" *I love seeing them interact and have fun with their friends and it is nice to be part of that and provide an environment that helps those friendships develop further."*

CHAPTER 9
Final Thoughts

We hope you have found the information in this book both positive and useful, that it has given you plenty to reflect on but crucially that there are things that you can take away and implement immediately to support the work that you are currently doing or about to begin.

Most importantly we want you to feel supported and valued in this amazing role that you take on.

You parent coaches are the bedrock of any sporting community and your role is vital for these sports programmes to continue to thrive and children to be given the opportunity to fall in love with sport and physical activity.

In those darker moments when you are upset or stressed with the role, never forget the huge number of lives that you may be positively impacting including that of your own children.

Keep checking in with your own child that it is a positive experience for them and be open enough to ask for their views. If your child is no longer enjoying the experience, then it may be time to think again. If it is not fun, it is no longer productive and the long-term relationship you have with your children is more important than the game itself.

Once the lights go out on the game and this part of your journey together, we hope that the impact on all of your lives has been a positive one, that you have created many happy memories and you have all grown positively as individuals.

Very few parents will coach their own children forever. There will come a time when you need to step away and just watch them play, hang up the 'Coaches hat' and devote your time to just being mum or dad and when it's time to let go (as their coach), let them go.

> **❝** *I feel like I can do stuff to help them which certainly make me feel better about my own parenting. At times it can be tough but this gives me an avenue to feel like I am really helping them."*

We hope that you have enjoyed this book. If you have, be sure to check out our other publications below for both parents and coaches.

Sign up and become a lifetime member of the WWPIS Platform today and access over 200 articles, videos and features in our high performance and parent zone covering a multitude of different topics.

For sporting parents, coaches and athletes a section written by Nino Severino, former British No. 1 tennis coach and member of Team GB for the 2012 Olympics.

The members area covers in depth the following components:

- Parent Support
- Mindset
- Strength and conditioning
- Performance Testing
- Nutrition
- Injury prevention
- Lifestyle
- Screening
- Training programmes
- Recovery
- Planning

For coaches there is 'Coaches Corner' where there are lots of supplementary resources for the book 'Engage' to support coaches with their parental engagement strategy.

BUY TODAY AT
WWW.PARENTSINSPORT.CO.UK